WJEC GCSE ENGLISH

ROGER LANE

FOUNDATION BOOK

ENGLISH
ENGLISH LITERATURE
ENGLISH LANGUAGE

WJEC
CBAC

OXFORD
UNIVERSITY PRESS

OXFORD
UNIVERSITY PRESS

Great Clarendon Street, Oxford OX2 6DP

Oxford University Press is a department of the University of Oxford.
It furthers the University's objective of excellence in research,
scholarship, and education by publishing worldwide in

Oxford   New York

Auckland   Cape Town   Dar es Salaam   Hong Kong   Karachi
Kuala Lumpur   Madrid   Melbourne   Mexico City   Nairobi
New Delhi   Shanghai   Taipei   Toronto

With offices in

Argentina   Austria   Brazil   Chile   Czech Republic   France   Greece
Guatemala   Hungary   Italy   Japan   Poland   Portugal   Singapore
South Korea   Switzerland   Thailand   Turkey   Ukraine   Vietnam

Oxford is a registered trade mark of Oxford University Press
in the UK and in certain other countries

British Library Cataloguing in Publication Data

Data available

ISBN 978-0-19-831083-9

10 9 8 7 6 5 4 3 2 1

Printed in Great Britain by Bell and Bain Ltd., Glasgow

Author's acknowledgements

Thanks to Nicola Dutton for her support and to Hayley
Cox and the team for all the professionalism in Oxford.
Thanks to Jay Shaw and Daniel Cox from Northfield
School, Oxford, for their work on the Literature tasks and
many thanks to George Hillesley for the article on Saint
Helena.

Mixed Sources
Product group from well-managed
forests and other controlled sources
www.fsc.org Cert no. TT-COC-002769
© 1996 Forest Stewardship Council
FSC

CONTENTS

INTRODUCTION

How to use this book if you are studying…

SECTION 1: READING

SECTION 2: WRITING

SECTION 3: SPEAKING AND LISTENING

How to use this book if you're studying
ENGLISH

Wherever you see this symbol , this means that the text and activities are matched to the **GCSE English specification**. Look out for the symbol in purple 'Your Assessment' panels, in 'Check your learning' boxes and alongside sample exam questions.

WJEC GCSE English is divided into four units. The grid below shows you which chapters cover the skills you need for each assessment.

Unit	Assessment	Related chapters
Unit 1: English in the Daily World (Reading)	**Exam lasting 1 hour.** Answer questions on two non-fiction texts. **AO2**	**Chapter 1.1** for reading non-fiction texts.
Unit 2: English in the Daily World (Writing)	**Exam lasting a 1 hour.** Complete two transactional or 'real-life' writing tasks. **AO3**	**Chapter 2.2** for transactional writing.
Unit 3: English in the World of the Imagination	**Controlled Assessment.**	
Section A: Literary Texts	**Section A:** Complete one task linking Shakespeare to literary heritage poetry and one task on a Different Cultures prose text. **AO2**	**Chapter 1.3** for reading poetry and Shakespeare. **Chapter 1.4** for studying Different Cultures prose.
Section B: Open Writing	**Section B:** Write one piece of first-person and one piece of third-person narrative writing. **AO3**	**Chapter 2.1** for narrative writing.
Unit 4: Speaking and Listening	**Controlled Assessment.** Complete three speaking and listening tasks. **AO1**	**Chapter 3.1** for speaking and listening.

How to use this book if you're studying

ENGLISH LANGUAGE

Wherever you see this symbol , this means that the text and activities are matched to the **GCSE English Language** specification. Look out for the symbol in purple assessment panels, in 'check your learning' boxes and alongside sample exam questions.

WJEC GCSE English Language is divided into four units. The grid below shows you which chapters cover the skills you need for each assessment.

Unit	Assessment	Related chapters
Unit 1: Studying written language	**Exam lasting 1 hour.** Answer questions on two non-fiction texts. **AO3**	**Chapter 1.1** for reading non-fiction texts.
Unit 2: Using written language	**Exam lasting a 1 hour.** Complete two transactional or 'real-life' writing tasks. **AO4**	**Chapter 2.2** for transactional writing.
Unit 3: Literary reading and creative writing	**Controlled Assessment.**	
Section A: Studying written language	**Section A:** Write an essay on a literary text. **AO3**	**Chapters 1.3**, **1.4** and **1.5** for studying literary texts.
Section B: Using language	**Section B:** Write one piece of descriptive writing and one piece of narrative writing. **AO4**	**Chapter 2.1** for descriptive and narrative writing.
Unit 4: Spoken Language	**Controlled Assessment.**	
Section A: Using Language	**Section A:** Complete three speaking and listening tasks. **AO1**	**Chapter 3.1** for speaking and listening.
Section B: Studying Spoken Language	**Section B:** Write an essay on spoken language. **AO2**	**Chapter 3.2** for studying spoken language.

How to use this book if you're studying
ENGLISH LITERATURE

Wherever you see this symbol, this means that the text and activities are matched to the **GCSE English Literature specification**. Look out for the symbol in purple assessment panels, in 'check your learning' boxes and alongside sample exam questions.

WJEC GCSE English Literature is divided into three units. The grid below shows you which chapters cover the skills you need for each assessment.

Unit	Assessment	Related chapters
Unit 1: Prose (different cultures) and poetry (contemporary)	**Exam lasting 2 hours.**	
Section A: Individual texts in context	Answer two questions on a different cultures prose text. **AO1, AO2, AO4**	**Chapter 1.4** for studying Different Cultures prose.
Section B: Comparative study	Compare two contemporary unseen poems. **AO1, AO2, AO3**	**Chapter 1.2** for comparing unseen poetry.
Unit 2a: Literary heritage drama and contemporary prose **OR** **Unit 2b: Contemporary drama and literary heritage prose**	**Exam lasting 2 hours.** Study two texts and answer two questions on each of them. **AO1, AO2, AO4**	**Chapter 1.5** for studying drama and prose.
Unit 3: Poetry and drama (literary heritage)	**Controlled Assessment.** Write an essay linking Shakespeare to literary heritage poetry. **AO1, AO2, AO3**	**Chapter 1.3** for reading poetry and Shakespeare.

FEATURES OF THIS BOOK

This book provides a range of useful features to help you find your way through the course. Here is a quick guide to what you will find:

- **Your Assessment** – these purple boxes appear at the start of each chapter and include a quick break-down of the Exam or Controlled Assessment covered in the chapter. This box also includes a checklist of the skills you will learn in the chapter. The colour-coded hand icons show you how this information relates to the subject you are studying, whether it is English, English Language or English Literature.

- **Examiner's Tips** – these blue tip boxes appear throughout the book and contain valuable pointers on where to pick up marks in each assessment. There are also some useful tips about 'what not to do' so you should pay attention to these too!

- **Exam/Controlled Assessment Practice** – you will find this section at the end of each chapter. It provides example questions based on real exam papers or Controlled Assessment tasks.

- **Sample Student Responses and Examiner's Comments** – this book provides you with a lots of sample answers from students along with feedback from an examiner. These comments explain what is required of you and can help you find ways to gain a higher mark.

- **Check your learning** – these panels ask you to rate your progress on a scale of 1 to 4. Answer the questions honestly to find out where you can improve.

- **Functional Skills** – some sections of this book are marked with a Functional Skills logo,  . These activities will help you to practise using Functional Skills in writing and speaking and listening.

Chapter 1.1

Non-Fiction Texts

Your Assessment

This chapter deals with the skills you need to read non-fiction texts, which include texts such as letters, leaflets, advertisements, magazine articles, reports, fact-sheets, biographies, diaries and blogs.

For GCSE English and GCSE English Language, you will be tested on reading non-fiction texts by an exam lasting **one hour**. In the exam, you will be given **two texts** and you will have to answer four questions on them. Some of the questions will ask you to look at one of the texts and one of the questions will ask you to use information from both texts in your answer.

Learn how to...

✔ identify the audience and purpose of each text you study

✔ find information in a text

✔ explain details from a text in your own words

✔ identify the writer's ideas and opinions in a text

✔ understand the effects of persuasive techniques

✔ make cross-references across two texts.

What are non-fiction texts?

Non-fiction texts include mostly everything that cannot be described as poetry, drama or a fictional story. They may be factual – but not always. Non-fiction texts include things like letters and emails as well as articles that you find on the Internet or in magazines and newspapers.

In your exam for this unit, you may be asked to answer questions on texts, such as:

You need to be aware of why different texts are written (the **purpose**) and who they are written for (the **audience**). You also need to be aware of what different texts look like (the **format**) and who the 'speaker' is (the **voice**).

EXAMINER'S TIP

■ When writing about non-fiction texts remember that you are being tested on your reading skills. Do not make empty points about headlines, pictures and columns! Make sure that what you are writing links to the meaning of the text.

> **Look carefully at the two texts below. Who do you think each text is aimed at? What is each text trying to do? Explain your answers.**

Inspire!
Become a leader

Are you 16–25 looking for just that bit more out of life? Love outdoor adventure and taking part in activities such as abseiling, skateboarding and kayaking?

Do you enjoy working with young people? Could you make a genuine difference?

Then this is for you

Scouting is a growing Movement. Volunteers make it all possible and there's never been a better time to become a leader.

Inspire others – call 0845 300 1818 or visit
www.scouts.org.uk/join

FIRE SAFETY IN THE HOME

Did you know…?

- You're twice as likely to die in a fire if you don't have a smoke alarm that works.
- 90 people die each year because the battery in their smoke alarm is flat or missing.

Smoke alarms are cheap and easy to install.

Get it. Install it. Check it. It could save your life.

FIRE KILLS
YOU **CAN** PREVENT IT

Can you find things in a text?

One of the first things you will be asked to do in your exam will be to read a text and pick out details from it. Read the short extract from a holiday brochure below.

> There is also plenty of entertainment for adults too. If granny and granddad need a break, we have daily bingo sessions, sing-alongs around our grand piano and tea dances three times a week. After all, we believe a holiday should please everyone, not just the children. For more adventurous adults, there are boat trips, steam engine journeys and even the chance to race go-karts like the kids!

List five activities that older people are offered in the text. Your list might begin:

Student response

1. bingo   5.

2. sing-alongs

3.

4.

Can you explain things in your own words?

As well as picking out pieces of information from a text, you also need to be able to show that you understand what a text is saying by putting it into your own words. Read the text below.

> Although conserving the planet is clearly a good thing and has very obvious benefits, we are constantly being made to feel guilty for putting out our wheelie bins each week. We seem to be driven to the point of going through our rubbish every day to ensure that a stray piece of lettuce leaf hasn't slipped into the bins instead of into the compost heap.

In your own words, explain what point is being made about wheelie bins, rubbish collections and saving the planet.

When you are asked this type of question you need to say it how it is. The passage above suggests that some recycling is a bit pointless, and won't make any real difference to the future of the planet. To worry about a small piece of lettuce falling into the wrong bin seems foolish.

Can you deal with persuasive techniques?

Writers of non-fiction texts will often do more than just supply information. They may also try to **persuade** you to do something or think something or just to agree with their opinions.

> **How does the headline below try to persuade people to visit the tourist attraction?**

"A unique and exciting day out for all the family." Discovering history you can see, feel and touch...

This headline claims to include an actual quotation, as if it's from a satisfied customer perhaps. Like nearly all attractions that are mentioned in advertisements, it does everything for everybody! The advert suggests the attraction is one of a kind (unique) and an exciting hands-on experience for both old and young visitors.

A writer may use a number of persuasive techniques in the same piece of writing. For example:

- quotations from other people
- statistics such as percentages
- language chosen to engage the senses
- attention-grabbing headlines.

The key to writing about persuasive techniques is to think back to the **purpose** of the text and explain **how** the writer uses particular techniques to achieve this purpose.

EXAMINER'S TIP

■ When commenting on headlines look at the words used rather than the appearance of them. In the headline above, 'unique' is the obvious word to pick for a comment – a much overused word these days, as lots of people claim things are 'unique', but are they really?

Look at the extracts below. For each extract:
- **identify what the writer's purpose is**
- **explain how the writer persuades the reader to think or act in a particular way.**

I'm writing to complain about the appalling level of cleanliness on the trains run by your company and I would like to insist that something is done about this as soon as possible. I catch the train every day in order to get to work, however, I have become increasingly disgusted by the amount of litter, food waste and general grime that I have to endure every time I use your service. If something is not done about this soon, I'm afraid I will be forced to reconsider using your trains in future.

Register with us now to claim your two FREE tickets. All you have to do is log on to the address below and enter your name, interests and email address to receive tickets to one of 100 participating cinemas across the UK. We will only contact you with offers matched to the interests you specify. It's that simple. Make sure you get your tickets – register with us today!

Did you know that each year food stores in the UK give out enough plastic bags to cover the surface of London? Most of these bags are buried in landfill sites where they then take between 500 and 1000 years to break down. Despite the damage this does to the environment, 20% of people still insist on having a new bag every time they shop. One in ten people take a bag only to throw it away immediately. What can be done to change this? Using a 'bag for life' is one way that you can make a difference.

I've seen both versions of the film and in my opinion the original was way more convincing. The remake is just all about fight scenes and special effects and the story has been stripped right down. The characters just aren't believable and I didn't get the ending. Why do so many film directors think we just want to watch explosions and gun fights? We've seen it all before and frankly it's getting pretty boring; give me the version with a story any day!

EXAMINER'S TIP

- Purpose and audience go hand in hand. Purpose provokes the questions, 'Why is the writer writing this? What is he or she up to?' In some texts the answer is more clear-cut than in others – so there could be more than one purpose to the writing.

Can you make cross-references across two texts?

In your exam, you will read two non-fiction texts, so you will need to practise making cross-references between them.

The following texts provide two views of Pembroke Castle in South Wales. The first text describes Pembroke Castle as it looks today, emphasizing what the historical site has to offer visitors. The second text mostly focuses on explaining the castle's history: why it was built and how it was damaged in later years.

Compare and contrast how the castle is described in both texts.

10 Idyllically set on the banks of the river estuary, this mighty fortress is largely intact, and its endless passages, tunnels and stairways are great fun to explore, plus there are super exhibitions, which tell the tale of its medieval life. Once the seat of a succession of major barons, this historic showpiece is the birthplace of Henry Tudor, father to the infamous Henry VIII and grandfather of Elizabeth I.

Spend a day, and picnic in the beautifully kept grounds and from the opposite bank of the river, view the castle in all its splendour, surrounded by a peaceful stretch of water.

11 In the Middle Ages, Pembroke was strategically important. It was one of the main ports for travelling to Ireland and the seat of the earls of Pembroke, with a castle that was one of the strongest in the kingdom. Both the town and the castle developed and were fortified together.

When Oliver Cromwell attacked the town in 1648 the walls of the castle were in good repair, allowing the inhabitants to withstand attack for some time. When surrender did eventually come, some lengths of the walls were demolished as a punishment. The castle never recovered from this blow.

Exam practice 1

Source text A
'Why can't we cope with snow?'

Whatever the weather, people in Britain seem to like to talk about it but there's nothing like a fall of snow to cause debate and controversy. The writer of this article from *The Guardian* asks the question in the headline, but really complains about the nation's inability to deal with a sudden, or not so sudden, spell of wintry weather.

Why can't we cope with snow?

Heavy snow fell across England and Wales this morning, and predictably, travel chaos was not far behind. "Adverse weather" led to closed airports, cancelled trains and caused a morning of travel misery for many Britons.

At least we can see the snow – it's more credible than leaves on the line – but really, honestly, we're looking at a few centimetres here, not metres. And we had plenty of prior warning.

Virgin trains blamed delays on "snow that had fallen, snow that was still falling as well as ice forming on overhead power lines."

While Network Rail explained that many of the London commuter trains that can't cope well with snow are run on third rail electrics. "Some trains are failing and breaking down," a spokesperson helpfully explained.

Snow which falls outside office hours is particularly unhelpful, it seems. "Snow can pose a threat to the railway if it ... continues to fall outside normal working hours," according to Network Rail.

As for the Tube – don't even go there. 'Severe delays' is the catchphrase of the day. A little snow goes a long way in causing havoc with signals.

And airports? We awoke to find Stansted, Luton, Birmingham and Cardiff closed. Was the snow at these hubs particularly vicious compared to say Gatwick or Heathrow? No one was able to enlighten me.

A spokeswoman at Birmingham Airport assured me that people had been out all night to clear the snow and that they had £750,000 worth of equipment on hand for snow-clearing operations. Which leaves me wondering why they still had to shut for two-and-a-half hours. Although they did better than Luton, which remained closed until midday with all flights suspended pending a runway inspection.

I did see someone skiing to work this morning, which looked a mite ambitious. And a little crazy. I suspect he was driven to it by one train cancellation too many.

Source text B

'Snow joke: Riot police rapped for sledding on shields'

This report from the *Belfast Telegraph* describes a prank carried out by police in the snow. It leaves the reader to decide what view to take of the sledding incident, or does it?

Snow joke: Riot police rapped for sledding on shields

Policemen in England filmed using a riot shield as a makeshift sledge have been reprimanded for the prank, a force has said.

A passer-by captured the moment Thames Valley Police officers arrived at the slope in Berkeley Road, Boars Hill, Oxford, in a riot van. One is then seen clambering on to the shield, advised by a colleague: "You've got to hold on to the straps."

Another officer appears to be filming the incident on his mobile phone as the policeman is pushed down the slope, to a shout of: "Whatever happens, keep smiling!"

He then travels down the hill towards a ditch, to the obvious amusement of his three colleagues watching.

Superintendent Andrew Murray, Oxford City commander with Thames Valley Police, said: "The snow has a habit of bringing out the child in all of us. I have spoken to the officers concerned and reminded them in no uncertain terms that tobogganing on duty, on police equipment and at taxpayers' expense is a very bad idea should they wish to progress under my command."

Rick Latham, who filmed the 41-second clip on Tuesday afternoon before posting it on the YouTube website, said he initially thought police were going to tell him off.

The 50-year-old, who was attempting to get down the slope in a kayak, said: "We were just having a laugh, then they pulled up and we thought they were going to give us a hard time.

Then they asked how slippy the snow was, and one of them grabbed the shield, then another one went down on it as well. I asked if I could film it and they said that was fine. They said something like: 'We're only human'."

Mr Latham said he was impressed by the officers' behaviour and hopes they were not severely reprimanded. He added: "You don't always build up the most positive image of the police but they broke the mould. They were chatty and pleasant. It was just nice to see them in that situation."

*Answer **all** the following questions.*

The Resource Material is from The Guardian *newspaper.*

The second article 'Snow joke: Riot police rapped for sledding on shields' is from the Belfast Telegraph.

Look at the article from *The Guardian* in the separate Resource Material.

1.   (i)   List **five** aspects of the snowy weather conditions that caused problems, according to the passage.   [5]

    (ii)   List **five** problems for the public caused by the snow, according to the passage.   [5]

2.   What is the writer's attitude to the snowy weather?   [10]

Now look at the article 'Snow joke: Riot police rapped for sledding on shields' on the opposite page.

3.   How does the writer keep you interested in 'Snow joke'?   [10]

You should now use details and information <u>from both texts</u> to answer the following question:

4.   Which of the two reports do you find more effective, and why?   [10]

This question may be presented in either one or two parts. It is not the most difficult question, but you should read the wording carefully and make sure that you do not repeat the same point twice.

This question asks you to explain the writer's viewpoint, so you need to select and organize the relevant information from the text effectively. You also need to put your answer into your own words.

The wording of this question prompts you to think about 'how' the writer persuades you to react in a particular way to the article. Be prepared to explain your personal reaction, but remember to write about why the writer makes you feel this way.

At least one of the questions on the exam paper will ask you to write about both texts. Aim to make your most important points first and try to write an equal amount about each text. Try to keep your paragraphs short and focused throughout your answer.

Each question on the exam paper for this unit will ask you to do something slightly different in order to test different reading skills. It is therefore important that you read the question wording very closely.

This section looks at a range of possible question types.

Search and find question

The first question on the exam paper is likely to be a 'search and find question', asking you to read one of the texts and pick out specific details. This question may be presented like the one below.

Look at the article from _The Guardian_ in the separate Resource Material.

1.   (i)   List **five** aspects of the snowy weather conditions that caused problems, according to the passage.   [5]

    (ii)   List **five** problems for the public caused by the snow, according to the passage.   [5]

Even though you should answer this type of question comfortably, do not treat it casually. The two-part question makes you think a little by forcing you to sort out the snow from the problems caused; in other words, the causes from the effects.

Remember also that this question is not intended to be a guessing game. Cold weather causes burst pipes in people's homes… but not in this text!

Read the 'Why can't we cope with snow?' article on page 15 again and complete the following activity to practise searching for and locating information in the text.

- ■ **Write a response to question 1(i) and 1(ii) above, presenting each answer in the form of a short list.**
- ■ **A similar question for this part of the exam could have been: 'What are the problems caused by the snow and the reasons for them?' In what ways would this question have been easier or harder to answer?**

Explaining and summarizing question

When answering this type of question you need to use your own words to reorganize the text, and you need to write fluently in clearly-constructed sentences.

---

2. What is the writer's attitude to the snowy weather? [10]

The question could also be worded:

What impressions of the travel and weather situation does the writer create?

Or: *What are the writer's thoughts and feelings about the heavy snow in England and Wales?*

All of these questions ask you to consider the writer's **viewpoint** or opinion on the subject matter of the article. You should look at the **tone** the writer uses. Is the writer understanding or does she seem surprised by the way the transport companies have reacted to the snow? How can you tell?

You should also look at the writer's **choice of language**. Why does the writer choose to use words such as 'particularly unhelpful' and 'particularly vicious'?

Read the example response to Question 2 below:

Student response

The writer doesn't like snow and doesn't like what happens to the country when it snows: 'honestly, we're looking at a few centimetres here, not metres'. The writer thinks that when we have a very small amount of snow 'a few centimetres', we suddenly have chaos, as all the airports and trains seem to stop, which means that people cannot get anywhere and everyone is miserable.

The writer thinks all the companies which are named in the passage – 'Virgin trains', 'Network Rail', 'the Tube', Birmingham and Luton airports – all came up with amazing excuses as to why they cannot operate due to snow. It has an impact on everything; signals, overhead cables, electrical breakdown, and the writer cannot understand why this would happen with only a small amount of snow. The writer says 'severe delays' is the catchphrase of the day and is very sarcastic about it, particularly in the last sentence, which reads: 'I suspect he was driven to it by one train cancellation too many'.

Now write your answer to Question 2, trying to get across the writer's strength of feeling.

Questions on the writer's techniques

A question on persuasive techniques does not necessarily have to have the word 'persuasion' in it. Be alert to what the writer of a text wants you to think – in other words, how a writer wants to influence you.

Look again at the 'Snow joke' article on page 16 and the question that relates to it below:

> **3.** How does the writer keep you interested in 'Snow joke'?   [10]

In the case of this article, most people will think that the police are the good guys, so what does the writer say and how does he or she say it? Read one student's response to the question below:

Student response

As soon as you see the title you are interested, as everyone likes to see something funny to do with the police and the action picture grabs your attention. You read on to see what the police were doing and what happens when they get told off. The writer also includes where the film can be seen and shows that their boss 'reminded them in no uncertain terms' that they shouldn't have been tobogganing when on duty, and also been seen by taxpayers which would not do them any good with the public. He also lets us know that the officers obviously had fun. The writer gives the comments of the person who filmed them and it is his nice comments that keep you reading and it can change your own opinion of the police when he says 'It was just nice to see them in that situation'.

This student begins successfully by giving his own response to the article but immediately backs this up with reference to features of the text. His point about the structure of the text is a valid one – the writer uses the headline and image as a hook and encourages the reader to read on to find out the fate of those involved.

What do you think the student could have done to make the answer more focused?

The 'writer's techniques' question on the 'Snow joke' article could also take the following form:

> *What are your thoughts and feelings on the policemen sledding and how does the writer create those thoughts and feelings?*

Or: *How does the writer try to make you sympathetic to the police in 'Snow joke'?*

Choose one of the questions above and write an answer to it, giving your own opinions freely, while using the details of the text to back up your views.

Comparison question

One question in this exam will always ask you to look at both of the texts provided. You should be ready for one of a range of approaches.

The task may be worded:

> *Compare and contrast…*

Or: *What are the similarities and differences…?*

Or: *Which of the texts do you think is more effective, and why?*

With any of these question types, you may be given bullet points to help you structure your answer. If so, use them! Keep your answer organized. Keep your sentences crisp and balanced.

Read the example comparative task below and the student response to it on the next page.

You should now use details and information <u>from both texts</u> to answer the following question:

4. Which of the two reports do you find more effective, and why? [10]

Both passages are aimed at the general public and are about snow and how it can affect you. The first passage shows that the snow can cause chaos and disruption to everyone, whereas the second one shows how it can be fun and enjoyable although still have consequences, when it shows the police getting into trouble because they were caught on camera.

Both passages have people called spokespeople giving opinions and comments. In the first passage people from Network Rail and Birmingham Airport are asked to comment on why the disruption is happening to cause the problems and, in the second, Superintendent Andrew Murray is quoted as to what he said to his officers.

Both passages do show humour although in different ways. In the first passage the writer is sarcastic about the snow, particularly the fact that it is such a small amount to do so much damage to everything, but in the second passage the humour is much more evident. The police and the public were just having a laugh and behaving like children.

Both passages make reference to unusual activity. The first one tells us that 'I did see someone skiing to work this morning' and the second tells us about police tobogganing and that one member of the public was going down the slope in a kayak, both unusual things to see in Great Britain.

- **Discuss the response with a partner. What do you think the student does well in the response?**
- **Write a further two paragraphs to this response adding two of your own points to the piece of writing.**

Exam practice 2

Source text A
'St Helena – a world apart'

St Helena Island (pronounced *saint he-lee-na*) is a remote island situated in the South Atlantic Ocean. The extract that follows is taken from a piece of autobiographical travel writing. In this extract the writer describes his experience as a visitor to the island.

St Helena – a world apart

We travelled south from Britain in the *HMS St Helena*, the supply boat that serves the island of St Helena. This boat is the sole means of supplying the island with goods from the outside world.

It held about 130 people, who were travelling between Britain, Ascension Island, St Helena and the Falkland Isles. Only about a dozen of us were tourists heading for St Helena. When we arrived there, after sailing for five days, docking was so difficult that elderly people such as ourselves had to be lifted off the boat on to the quayside in a cage, six at a time.

The island is only 50 square miles, about 10 miles long and 5 miles wide, and all of the roads are single lane. There is a population of only about five thousand and they speak with a very strong English dialect. It's one of the most racially mixed communities I have ever seen, because over the centuries South Africans, Indians, Portuguese and others have stopped off there and settled. Everyone is very friendly, and you are likely to be stopped in the street with 'How you? Who you is? Is you going walk? See you.'

Our hotel was the best on the island, but it was still a straightforward, no-frills place to stay. Socially, we witnessed a lively drink-up on the Friday night when locals collected at

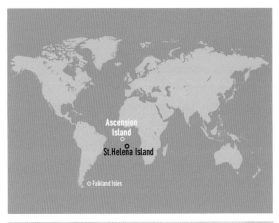

The Island of St Helena is 10.5 miles long and 6.5 miles wide consisting of a steep, rocky terrain.

our hotel. Life on the island goes on with a golf club and an Olympic-sized swimming pool as obvious sporting attractions. The locals also play a lot of cricket.

We went around the island chauffeured in an open-top 1929 Chevrolet. The driver had to stop to put the roof up if it started to rain, which it did quite frequently when we were there. It was hot, damp and murky for much of the time. On our tour, we saw Diana's Park, the highest point on St Helena, a national park with protected rare trees. We also saw the Heart-shaped Waterfall, which cascades through the middle of a heart-shaped cliff face and High Knoll Fort, built in readiness for an invasion of the island.

Of course, Napoleon spent his last few years as a British prisoner on the island and died there. Longwood House, where he lived in exile, is now owned by the French government, and a rather miserable Frenchman was in charge when we visited. Napoleon's Tomb is a tourist attraction, even though Napoleon's remains have been returned to France. We also saw Government House, a big building for such a small island, and the great turtle, over 170 years old!

There has been talk of an airport for the island for years, and most of the islanders would want it. Unfortunately, even a primitive airstrip would cost roughly the same as a new supply boat for the island, and they probably need both.

The shops in Jamestown, the only town on the island, are also very primitive. People stock-up expertly every few weeks when the boat brings new supplies. Some of the islanders walk down the famous Jacob's Ladder, all 699 steps, to the shops and back up again with their bags. Shoppers have to pay British prices, but islanders in employment can earn only a fraction of a UK salary.

Jacob's Ladder – built in 1829 to haul goods up and down from the island capital. It has 699 steps and stretches 600 feet high.

In the old days, perhaps a thousand ships a year would call at St Helena, but now apart from the supply boat every few weeks it's just the odd cruise ship and racing yachts for a few hours as they cross the Atlantic.

Young people want to leave the island, but not all of them want it to have an airport. Some of them are loyal to the traditional view that the island's uniqueness will be lost if the airport is built. They wish the island to remain the same, so that they can retire back to it. More to the point, though, the airport is not a practical proposition. It is hard to see a bright future for St Helena.

Source text B
'Join the Airport for St Helena Group'

People far and wide who have an interest in St Helena have joined a campaign for an airport to be built on the island to improve access. This campaign website argues the case for it and attempts to widen support for the airport.

http://www.airportforhelena.com

JOIN THE AIRPORT FOR ST HELENA GROUP

The British Government has brought the St Helena airport construction project to a halt.

The airport is vital to reduce the isolation of over 4,000 inhabitants who are loyal British citizens. It would give them and thousands of other 'Saints' in the UK and other countries hope for a better future.

St Helena has changed in recent years from the paradise of past memories. Life is becoming increasingly desperate for many people. There are only limited opportunities for skilled workers and young people, many of whom are being forced to leave their families to seek work abroad. Over a hundred and fifty children and young adults are now in informal foster care as a result.

The close family unit on which St Helena prided itself is fast breaking down. The population is now increasingly comprised

http://www.airportforhelena.com

of the elderly and children. Consequently, income will continue to decrease, the island will become more dependent on British Aid and it will become more and more isolated and fall into economic decline.

An airport provides the only real hope of developing tourism and other businesses. A sustainable high-value, low-volume tourism industry would inject cash into the community. Negative impacts would be minimal. The people need this to survive. Saints do not want UK handouts. Being able to provide for themselves would restore pride and motivation to their community.

The airport project has been planned for over six years and was scheduled to be completed by 2012. It had galvanized islanders to plan for a future of self-sufficiency after years of steady decline. Whilst the island is grateful for the many years it's been served by the *HMS St Helena*, sea access alone has not stimulated economic development; nor will it in future. The *HMS* is also increasingly expensive to maintain and will need to be replaced in a few years at considerable cost.

THANK YOU FOR YOUR SUPPORT!

You can help in the following ways:

IF YOU LIVE IN THE UK:
Write to your Member of Parliament and ask them to support 'Airport for the Island of St Helena'.

IF YOU LIVE ON ST HELENA:
Sign the petition now being circulated on the island.

IF YOU ARE RESIDENT ELSEWHERE OVERSEAS:
Write to your British Government Representative in support of the airport.

*Answer **all** the following questions.*

The Resource Material *contains two separate texts. The first text is a piece of autobiographical travel writing about a visit to the Island of St Helena.*

The second text 'Join the Airport for St Helena Group' appeared on the Internet.

Look at the extract entitled 'St Helena – a world apart' in the separate Resource Material.

1. List **ten** things that tourists could do and see on the Island of St Helena. [10]

2. What impressions of St Helena does the writer give in his account? How does he create these impressions? [10]

Now look at 'Join the Airport for St Helena Group'.

3. How does the webpage try to persuade the reader to support the campaign for an airport on St Helena?
    You should consider:
    *   what is said about St Helena and Britain
    *   what is said about the changes in St Helena
    *   what is said about the airport itself
    *   the way the webpage is written and organized. [10]

To answer the next question you will need to look at <u>both texts</u>.

4. Which of these two texts do you find more effective in making readers interested in St Helena, and why? [10]
    You should organize your answer in paragraphs, and write about each of the following:
    *   the island as a place for tourists to visit
    *   the people of St Helena in each text
    *   the issue of the airport in each text
    *   the way the texts are written.

Focus on the key words of the question – what 'tourists could do or see'. Go through the text quickly, but methodically, and list your answers in bullet points. Keep your answers as short as possible and avoid copying out chunks of text.

An impression is an idea, opinion or thought. What are the writer's impressions? Are they good or bad, or a mixture of both? Explain 'how' the writer creates these impressions by picking out words from the text and using these as evidence. Try to write between five and six sentences to give yourself a chance to earn high marks out of ten.

Look at both texts for an answer to this question. You should look for one or two balanced, comparative comments per bullet point. Your opinion is invited by this question so don't be afraid to give it. However, always back this up with reference to the texts.

To answer this question, try to pick out interesting features, comments and arguments. Look for persuasive words and phrases and comment on them. Write a short paragraph for each of the bullet points provided in the question and avoid vague comments.

Sample answers

Here is a set of answers written by one student followed by comments from the examiner.

Student response Question 1

1. go to the golf club
2. go to the Olympic-sized swimming pool
3. play cricket with the local people
4. go sightseeing
5. see Diana's Park – the highest point
6. see the Heart-shaped Waterfall
7. see High Knoll Fort
8. go to the shops
9. see where Napoleon is buried
10. see the great turtle

EXAMINER'S COMMENT

This answer is almost there; however, there are a few inaccuracies which suggest this student may have rushed his or her reading. The writer mentions visiting Napoleon's Tomb but not 'the place where Napoleon is buried'. He is actually buried in France! Also, there are one or two generalizations; for example 'go sightseeing' is quite vague. The question is testing your ability to pick out details, so you should always be specific.

Student response Question 2

The writer gives an impression of St Helena as a lonely place that is cut off from the rest of the world. He says that the boat they use to get to the island is the 'sole means of supplying the island' with goods from elsewhere. He also describes the island as small with a small population of '130 people'. This gives an impression of a very tiny island. In addition to this, the writer also notices the basic conditions of life on St Helena. He says the shops are 'primitive' and the hotel is a 'no-frills place to stay'. There doesn't seem to be that many luxuries on the island. But the people on the island seem to be lively and friendly, getting involved in drinking and playing cricket. The writer sums-up, however, by showing his concern for the future of the island. With fewer people visiting and no plans to make transport easier with an airport, he says that 'it is hard to see a bright future for St Helena'. This creates the impression that life on the island is likely to get harder as time goes by.

EXAMINER'S COMMENT

This response deals very well with the first part of the question – explaining the impressions given by the writer – but it does not spend as much time investigating how the writer conveys these impressions. What is it about the writer's choice of language that makes the island seem lonely and isolated? This student selects quotations from the text effectively, but needs to comment on them in more detail. When responding to this type of question remember that the 'how' is just as important as the 'what', and you should tackle both in your answer.

The website persuades the reader to get involved because it shows how difficult things are for the people who live on the island. The writer describes how children are having to leave their families behind to find a better life. The writer knows that most people would not like this to happen to their families, so this persuades them to help.

The writer explains how things are changing by becoming worse. The writer says, 'income will continue to decrease' and 'it will become more and more isolated'. This suggests that time is running out for the people on the island, and unless the airport is built soon, things will keep going downhill.

The writer calls the airport 'the only real hope of developing tourism and other businesses'. The words 'only real hope' stress how important the airport is as they show there is no other way forward. This is persuasive because it makes the airport seem like the only option. The reasons for the airport are broken down into chunks, so it is easy for the reader to read them and build a clear picture of what problems the people face.

EXAMINER'S COMMENT

This answer is much stronger. The student has obviously thought carefully about 'how' the writer makes the reader think in a particular way. The points are well backed up with references to the text and there is some analysis of specific language choices. The student has also successfully followed the bullet-point list in the question to organize the response. He or she could have perhaps said more about the structure of the webpage, but overall this is a good answer.

I think the first text is the most interesting because the writer describes what it's like to actually be on the island first-hand. He gives details such as what the weather is like and what the people sound like. He describes the weather as 'hot, damp and murky for much of the time' and the people have 'a very strong English dialect'. These details keep the reader interested because they can imagine what it's like to actually be on the island.

The second text keeps the reader interested in other ways, by getting them to take notice of problems on the island and carry on reading to find out what they can do to help. This text is more about what the problems are for people living on the island. The first text also mentions this, 'It is hard to see a bright future for St Helena', but this is not set out as clearly as in the second text. People are likely to be more interested in the situation if they know about what can be done. The website clearly sets this out by explaining that, 'you can help in the following ways' with a blue panel.

Both texts use statistics to interest the reader. I like the statistic about Jacobs Ladder, because this seems like such a weird thing to actually see. The statistics used in the webpage work in a different way by adding power to the argument. The campaign seems more important because it will help to stop the 'isolation of over 4,000 inhabitants' and stop hundreds of children having to leave their families.

In my opinion the first text is the most effective at keeping the reader interested because it has a wider range of details about the island. The second text is also effective too, however, in different ways – by keeping people focused on the airport campaign and showing them how to get involved.

EXAMINER'S COMMENT

This answer includes a good balance of the student's personal opinions and close references to each text. This student is skilful at writing about both texts together, rather than one at a time, which means that the points of comparison seem tighter. There is also equal coverage of both texts, which is a good thing to aim for.

The answer could be improved by closer reference to particular language choices. What is it about the words used in the second text, for example, that makes the campaign seem so urgent?

How is non-fiction reading assessed at GCSE?

Use the questions below to check your level of performance when responding to tasks on non-fiction texts.

Search and find question (Question 1)

This question type tests your ability to read and understand texts and pick out relevant details.

Are there…
- ❏ some relevant points, which are presented as chunks of text copied from the extract?
- ❏ some relevant points, arranged as a bullet-point list?
- ❏ a good selection of carefully chosen points, but not quite enough to answer the question?
- ❏ a good selection of carefully chosen points that satisfy the exact requirements of the question?

Explaining and summarizing question (Question 2)

This kind of question also tests your ability to read and understand texts, but you will need to explain the writer's opinions and ideas too. You will need to present your answer as a continuous piece of writing, so you will be tested on your ability to select and organize information.

Are there…
- ❏ some points with chunks of copying from the text?
- ❏ relevant points with references to the text and some comment?
- ❏ valid points backed up with evidence from the text and effective comment?
- ❏ well-organized and valid points, backed up with evidence and effective comment?

Questions on the writer's techniques (Question 3)

This kind of question tests your understanding of writers' techniques and how they use these to influence the reader.

Are there…
- ❏ some points about the effects of the text but mostly paraphrasing?
- ❏ some points about the effects of the text and how the writer achieves them?
- ❏ valid comments about the effects of the text and reference to exactly what the writer does to achieve them?
- ❏ valid comments about the effects of certain features of the text, all supported with well-selected evidence?

> **Comparison question (Question 4)**
> This question type tests your ability to compare and contrast two texts and make cross-references between them.
>
> Are there…
> ❏ points about both texts but limited links between them?
> ❏ some cross-references and contrasts but evidence of more time spent writing about one of the texts?
> ❏ valid cross-references and contrasts between texts and a balanced approach to both of them?
> ❏ well-selected contrasts and cross-references dealing with both texts, backed up with evidence and organized effectively?

Preparing for the exam

Here is a break down of the key information from the GCSE specifications for this part of the assessment, including the Assessment Objectives for each specification (these are the skills that you need to show to gain marks).

GCSE ENGLISH UNIT 1: English in the daily world (reading)

Reading: non-fiction texts (20%)

Examination

You will complete questions on **two** non-fiction texts. The exam will last for **one** hour.

AO2 Reading

- Read and understand texts, selecting material appropriate to purpose, collating from different sources and making comparisons and cross-references as appropriate.
- Develop and sustain interpretations of writers' ideas and perspectives.
- Explain and evaluate how writers use linguistic, grammatical, structural and presentational features to achieve effects and engage and influence the reader.
- Understand texts in their social, cultural and historical contexts.

GCSE ENGLISH LANGUAGE UNIT 1: Studying written language

Reading: non-fiction texts (20%)

Examination

You will complete questions on **two** non-fiction texts. The exam will last for **one** hour.

AO3 Studying written language

- Read and understand texts, selecting material appropriate to purpose, collating from different sources and making comparisons and cross-references as appropriate.
- Develop and sustain interpretations of writers' ideas and perspectives.
- Explain and evaluate how writers use linguistic, grammatical, structural and presentational features to achieve effects and engage and influence the reader.
- Understand texts in their social, cultural and historical contexts.

Before the day

- Revise different types of text to cover those which might appear in the exam.
- Look at as many 'past papers' and 'specimen papers' as you can.
- Look at example questions and highlight key words, such as those which ask you to consider writers' thoughts and feelings or persuasive techniques.
- Practise answering separate questions from practice exam papers for this unit in timed conditions; you should also attempt a complete exam paper.

On the day

- Read the texts and questions first before you answer anything – read quickly but purposefully.
- Work out what the audience and purpose is for each text.
- Work out the writer's attitudes in each of the texts.
- Annotate the texts as you read and underline key words.
- Focus closely on what each question is asking you to do – is it a 'how' or a 'what' question?
- Spend more or less equal time on each question (12–13 minutes each).
- Write answers of more or less equal length.
- Do not miss out any questions!

Check your learning...

Now that you have reached the end of this chapter, look at the list of points below and give yourself a rating of 1 to 4 for each one. '1' means that you still have work to do on this skill, while '4' means that you can perform this skill very well.

Can you...

- ✔ identify the audience and purpose of a text by reading it?
- ✔ find things in a text and pick out details?
- ✔ explain texts in your own words and describe the opinions expressed by the writer?
- ✔ identify persuasive techniques and explain how they work?
- ✔ make cross-references and comparisons across two texts?

Your Assessment

In this exam, you have to write about two poems on the same topic and compare them. These poems will be **contemporary**, which simply means that they have been written in recent times about modern life. The poems will also be **unseen**, which means you will not know what they will be until you open your exam paper, where they will be printed along with the exam question. You will have **one hour** to complete your response.

This chapter covers the skills you need to respond to unseen poetry. It also looks at how to structure and write a comparison.

Learn how to...

✔   identify the voice and situation in the poems you read
✔   write sensibly about poems you have seen for the first time
✔   pick out details to support your points
✔   build your personal view into your response
✔   compare and contrast two poems.

Reading a poem you haven't seen before

When you read a poem for the first time, try to get an overall sense of what it is about. Don't be put off if you don't understand every last word and detail. Poems are often written to encourage readers to think and work things out. A good place to start with any poem is to think about the **voice** and **situation**.

The 'voice' is the speaker in the poem. From whose perspective is the poem written? Is it a first-person or a third-person speaker? Does the voice have any particular characteristics, such as an angry or sad tone? How would you describe the attitude of the voice?

The 'situation' is the subject-matter of the poem. What happens in it? What does it describe? What ideas is it trying to put across to you?

Read the poem 'Woman Work' by Maya Angelou on the next page. What can you say about the voice and situation in this poem?

Woman Work

I've got the children to tend
The clothes to mend
The floor to mop
The food to shop
5   Then the chicken to fry
The baby to dry
I got company to feed
The garden to weed
I've got shirts to press
10 The tots to dress
The cane to be cut
I gotta clean up this hut
Then see about the sick
And the cotton to pick.

15 Shine on me, sunshine
Rain on me, rain
Fall softly, dewdrops
And cool my brow again.

Storm, blow me from here
20 With your fiercest wind
Let me float across the sky
'Til I can rest again

Fall gently, snowflakes
Cover me with white
25 Cold icy kisses and
Let me rest tonight.

Sun, rain, curving sky
Mountain, oceans, leaf and stone
Star shine, moon glow
30 You're all that I can call my own.

Maya Angelou

What stands out in this poem? What do you find particularly effective or interesting about it? You could comment on certain words, images or the way the poem is organized.

Below are two openings from responses written about 'Woman Work'. Both students write sensibly about the poem despite having never seen it before. Both students would get credit for what they have written.

Student response 1

The poem is describing the woman's typical day and her attitudes towards it. Her typical day seems to consist of feeding the children, mending things, and cleaning, also cooking. All she longs to do is rest; she wants to be warm but cool, wet but dry. The weather seems to be her escape from her working day and something that she can call her own...

Discuss with a partner. If you were the examiner, what would you give credit for in the response above? What is the response less clear about?

Student response 2

This poem can be split into two parts, the first verse and the last five. The first verse reads very quickly and is just a list of jobs the woman does; it seems she has her hands full, but most of the jobs are normal, everyday, but some aren't - 'The cane to be cut... ...And the cotton to pick.'

The response above takes a different approach. Like the previous one, it is not perfect, but what does this student do well?

EXAMINER'S TIP

■ You might have an opinion on which of these efforts you like best, and why, but the real question perhaps ought to be: 'which one will be able to carry the writing on most successfully?'

When writing about unseen poetry, you should avoid starting out with a long introduction; it is better to get to grips with the poems straight away. You should also make sure that you start as you mean to go on – with a clear focus and a sense of direction in your writing.

Read and enjoy the two poems that follow. The first poem is by a football-mad poet from Barnsley, Ian McMillan. It is about supporting England during a big summer tournament.

In the End, it's the Hope...

Each time they play we always think
It'll be like 1966;
And it might be the crowd and it might be the drink
As the voices raise and the glasses clink
5   And the tactics fail and the passing stinks
But each time they play we always think
It'll be like 1966
But the game is a mess and nobody clicks
And nothing connects when the players kick
10 And you feel slightly cheated and a little bit sick
And it's nothing like 1966;

'Cos in the end, it's the hope that defeats you;
In the end, it's the hope that deflates
In the end the expectation's more than you can bear
15 As you watch the match from behind your chair
With your dad and six of your weeping mates
And you punch the wall and you tear your hair
Because the hope is more than you can bear
And it's nothing like 1966
20 When they're running like chickens and heading like bricks

So here's my advice: assume they'll lose
When you've sung the Anthem, sing the blues
Pretend you're watching Rochdale, Barnsley
Peterborough Pompey Hull or Bury;
25 'Cos football's up and down like a channel ferry
And you're sometimes miserable and sometimes merry
If you don't build 'em up you can't knock 'em down
And if your goalie's a fool and your striker's a clown
And your midfield's toiling and your manager's thick
30 And It's not too much like 66...
Expect nothing. Expect nothing. That's McMillan's Law
Then you'll be really happy with a nil-nil draw...

Ian McMillan

It's safe to say that Ian McMillan is 'speaking' in the poem as an England football supporter. Explore what he is saying and how he is saying it by answering the questions below.

> 1. **What is the situation that Ian McMillan explains in the poem?**
> 2. **The poem is divided into three sections or 'stanzas'. Explain what each of the stanzas is saying.**
> 3. **Which details of the poem bring it to life for you particularly?**
> 4. **What is Ian McMillan saying to readers at the end of the poem?**

The second poem is about turkeys at Christmas. It is by Benjamin Zephaniah, a poet who is well known as someone who is not a meat-eater.

Talking Turkeys

Be nice to yu turkeys dis christmas
Cos' turkeys just wanna hav fun
Turkeys are cool, turkeys are wicked
An every turkey has a Mum.
5 Be nice to yu turkeys dis christmas,
Don't eat it, keep it alive,
It could be yu mate, an not on your plate
Say, Yo! Turkey I'm on your side.
I got lots of friends who are turkeys
10 An all of dem fear christmas time,
Dey wanna enjoy it, dey say humans
   destroyed it
An humans are out of dere mind,
Yeah, I got lots of friends who are turkeys
15 Dey all hav a right to a life,
Not to be caged up an genetically made up
By any farmer an his wife.

Turkeys just wanna play reggae
Turkeys just wanna hip-hop
20 Can yu imagine a nice young turkey saying,
'I cannot wait for de chop',
Turkeys like getting presents,
   dey wanna watch christmas TV,
Turkeys hav brains an turkeys feel pain
25 In many ways like yu an me.

I once knew a turkey called... Turkey
He said "Benji explain to me please,
Who put de turkey in christmas
An what happens to christmas trees?",
30 I said "I am not too sure turkey
But it's nothing to do wid Christ Mass
Humans get greedy an waste more dan
   need be
An business men mek loadsa cash".

35 Be nice to yu turkey dis christmas
Invite dem indoors fe sum greens
Let dem eat cake an let dem partake
In a plate of organic grown beans,
Be nice to yu turkey dis christmas
40 An spare dem de cut of de knife,
Join Turkeys United an dey'll be delighted
An yu will mek new friends 'FOR LIFE'.

Benjamin Zephaniah

Think about what stands out about the poet's **voice** in the poem and the **situation** he describes as you answer the questions below.

> 1. **What is the writer's point of view in this poem and how is this expressed?**
> 2. **The poem is divided into four stanzas. Read each stanza again carefully and say what point is being made in each one.**
> 3. **What reaction do you think the poet is hoping to get from people reading this poem?**
> 4. **How successful is this poem in your opinion?**

Selecting details to support your points

Having identified what a poem is about and who is speaking, your next move should be to focus on the details. This means picking out words that you think are particularly effective or identifying images that work especially well. Remember to focus on what **effects** these create. Be prepared to give your own opinions – what do **you** think and why?

As you explore a poem in detail, you should get into the habit of using **annotation**. This simply means reading with a pen in your hand and making short notes by circling or underlining key phrases. You can use this technique to note down and sort out your thoughts on the poems. For example:

> *Talking Turkeys*
>
> Be nice to yu turkeys dis christmas
>
> Cos turkeys just <u>wanna hav fun</u> ←—*tone is light-hearted*
>
> Turkeys are cool, turkeys are wicked
>
> An <u>every turkey has a Mum.</u> ←—*makes turkeys seem more like people*

Imagery

As well as word choices you might also comment on the **imagery** within a poem. An image in poetry (or any other type of writing) is a picture created in the mind of the reader by the poet's words.

Images may be **descriptive** – helping you to imagine what something looks, sounds, or tastes like; or an image might suggest a **deeper meaning** – bringing to mind a particular feeling or referring to a wider theme.

Writing about poetry

When writing about poems, you should back up your ideas by including short quotations in your answer. Make sure your quotations support the points you are trying to make and try to show what they **reveal** about the poem.

Look back at 'In the End, it's the Hope…' by Ian McMillan on page 39. Make close reference to the text when answering the questions below.

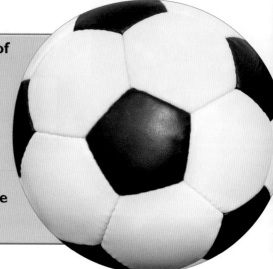

> 1. How does the poet's use of repetition add to the tone of the poem? What does it reveal about what it is like to be a football fan?
> 2. What do you notice about the poet's choice of language? How does it affect the overall mood of the poem? Select some examples to support your view.
> 3. What words does the rhyme help to draw your attention to? Does the rhyme pattern contribute to the tone of the poem? How?

Now take a second look at 'Talking Turkeys' by Benjamin Zephaniah on page 40. Use your close-reading skills to explore the poem in more detail.

> 1. Why do you think the poet chose the title 'Talking Turkeys'? How does the poet give turkeys a voice in this poem?
> 2. How would you describe the tone of the poem? Light-hearted or serious? Select words that create this impression and explain how they work.
> 3. What do you think the poet means by the phrase 'FOR LIFE' at the end of the poem? Could this phrase have more than one meaning?

EXAMINER'S TIP

■ When writing about poetry, you should avoid feature-spotting, for example: 'The writer has some good alliteration on line 3.' This will not gain you any marks! You should, however, write about what poems mean and how they work.

Comparing poems

Your study of poetry in this unit will require you to carry out a **comparison**. This means you will study two poems and consider how they are similar and different.

> **Look back at 'In the End, it's the Hope...' on page 39 and 'Talking Turkeys' on page 40. Can you find any similarities between these poems?**
> **Think about:**
> - **what the poems are about**
> - **the voice of each poet**
> - **the style of language used**
> - **the effect of each poem on the reader.**

Read and discuss the two poems that follow, making comparisons naturally as you go. Use the sample exam question, below, to guide your thinking. After you have read the poems once, work on them in detail, using the skills you have practised so far in this chapter.

SECTION B

Spend about 1 hour on this section. Think carefully about the poems before you write your answer.

6.   Both of the following poems, Playgrounds and Only the Wall, deal with victimization at school. The first looks at what it's like to feel like an outsider, while the second depicts the violent actions of a group of bullies.

   Write about both poems and their effect on you. Show how they are similar and how they are different.

   You may write about each poem separately and then compare them, or make comparisons where appropriate in your answer as a whole.

   You may wish to include some or all of these points:
   - *the content of the poems – what they are about;*
   - *the ideas the poet may have wanted us to think about;*
   - *the mood or atmosphere of the poems;*
   - *how they are written – words and phrases you find interesting, the way they are organized, and so on;*
   - *your responses to the poems.*   [20]

Playgrounds

Playgrounds are such gobby places.
Know what I mean?
Everyone seems to have something to
Talk about, giggle, whisper, scream and shout
    about,
5   I mean, it's like being in a parrot cage.

And playgrounds are such pushy places.
Know what I mean?
Everyone seems to have to
Run about, jump, kick do cartwheels,
    handstands, fly around,
10 I mean, it's like being inside a whirlwind.

And playgrounds are such patchy places.
Know what I mean?
Everyone seems to
Go round in circles, lines and triangles,
    coloured shapes,
15 I mean, it's like being in a kaleidoscope.

And playgrounds are such pally places.
Know what I mean?
Everyone seems to
Have best friends, secrets, link arms, be in
    gangs.
20 Everyone, except me.

Know what I mean?

Berlie Doherty

Only the Wall

That first day
only the wall saw
the bully
trip the new boy
5 behind the shed,
and only the wall heard
the name he called,
a name that would stick
like toffee.

10 The second day
the wall didn't see
the fight
because too many
boys stood around,
15 but the wall heard
their cheers,
and no one cheered for
the new boy.

The third day
20 the wall felt
three bullies
lean against it,
ready to ambush
the new boy,
25 then the wall heard
thumps and cries,
and saw blood.

The fourth day
only the wall missed
30 the new boy
though five bullies
looked for him,
then picked another boy
instead. Next day
35 they had him back,
his face hit the wall.

The sixth day
only the wall knew
the bullies
40 would need that other boy
to savage.
The wall remembered
the new boy's face
going home,
45 saw he'd stay away.

Matthew Sweeney

Look at the following notes from a student response on 'Playgrounds' and 'Only the Wall'. Which of the comments do you agree with and why?

Student response

Playgrounds

This poem appears to be about how nice and fun a playground is. It talks about the talk, the games and the colours and shapes.

The poem starts off in a happy mood but the last lines are said sadly.

It is something everyone can identify with as everyone went to school. I almost feel sorry for the poet but wonder why she was excluded.

Only the Wall

This poem is about bullies who get away with everything; nobody sees it except a wall. The poet would want bullies to understand what it would feel like to be bullied constantly.

The whole poem is based on the wall being the only thing to witness what is happening, showing that nobody really sees what goes on – as people say 'Nobody sees what really goes on behind those walls'.

How could you build some of these points into a comparison? What would you add to them?

A good way to approach your comparison is to focus on one poem in the first part of your answer and then move on to write about the second poem, making links back to the first poem where they occur to you. If you take this approach, you need to make sure that you spend an equal amount of time on each poem. You can use the bullet points provided in the exam question to help you structure your writing.

When writing a comparison you don't have to compare every single feature of the first poem with the second. It is more important that you read both poems and focus on both of them in detail when you write. If you do this you will find any differences between them as you build your response.

Now write a response to the exam question provided on page 43 referring to 'Playgrounds' and 'Only the Wall'. Attempt the exam question under time pressure. In other words, you should aim to complete your response in one hour.

Use the 'survival kit' below to help you put together a successful answer.

SURVIVAL KIT

- Allow **one hour** for the task.
- Read both poems to get a general fix on each one.
- Concentrate on the first poem, getting a clear sense of the voice and the situation of the poem.
- Read the poem in detail, sentence-by-sentence if you can, keeping an eye open for possible quotes, comments and ideas.
- Now work on the second poem, making comparisons with the first poem when you feel there is something worth saying.
- Round up the writing with any concluding comments you might have about each poem; a personal preference, for example.

EXAMINER'S TIP

■　When you compare two poems, do not use the ping-pong approach! In other words, do not go backwards and forwards between the poems on every point. For example: 'Poem A this, Poem B that, Poem A, Poem B...' and so on.

Exam practice

The following practice exam question includes two more poems to study and compare.

SECTION B

Spend about 1 hour on this section. Think carefully about the poems before you write your answer.

6.   Both of the following poems are about friendship. *About Friends* focuses on one specific friendship, while *Sometimes it happens* considers different relationships.

Write about both poems and their effect on you. Show how they are similar and how they are different.

You may write about each poem separately and then compare them, or make comparisons where appropriate in your answer as a whole.

You may wish to include some or all of these points:
- *the content of the poems – what they are about;*
- *the ideas the poet may have wanted us to think about;*
- *the mood or atmosphere of the poems;*
- *how they are written – words and phrases you find interesting, the way they are organized, and so on;*
- *your responses to the poems.*   [20]

About Friends

The good thing about friends
is not having to finish sentences.

I sat a whole summer afternoon with my friend once
on a river bank, bashing heels on the baked mud
and watching the small chunks slide into the water
and listening to them – plop plop plop.
He said 'I like the twigs when they… you know…
like that.' I said 'There's that branch…'

We both said 'Mmmm.' The river flowed and flowed
and there were lots of butterflies, that afternoon.

I first thought there was a sad thing about friends
when we met twenty years later.
We both talked hundreds of sentences,
taking care to finish all we said,
and explain it all very carefully,
as if we'd been discovered in places
we should not be, and were somehow ashamed.

I understood then what the river meant by flowing.

Brian Jones

Sometimes it happens

And sometimes it happens that you are friends and then
You are not friends
And friendship has passed.
And whole days are lost and among them
A fountain empties itself.

And sometimes it happens that you are loved and then
You are not loved,
And love is past.
And whole days are lost and among them
A fountain empties itself into the grass.

And sometimes you want to speak to her and then
You do not want to speak,
Then opportunity has passed.
Your dreams flare up, they suddenly vanish.

And also it happens that there is nowhere to go and then
There is somewhere to go,
Then you have bypassed.
And the years flare up and are gone,
Quicker than a minute.

So you have nothing.
You wonder if these things matter and then
As soon as you begin to wonder if these things matter
They cease to matter,
And caring is past.
And a fountain empties itself into the grass.

Brian Patten

How is the unseen poetry comparison assessed at GCSE?

Coverage of poems

❏ Are there simple, general comments on the poems?
❏ Is there some awareness of the mood, atmosphere and themes of the poems, as well as some discussion of these features?
❏ Is there focused and thoughtful discussion of the detail of both poems?
❏ Does the writing show appreciation of the poems and a clear analysis of them?

Comparisons

❏ Are there simple and basic points of comparison?
❏ Is there some awareness of similarities and differences, as well as further discussion of these points?
❏ Are the points of comparison made clearly and purposefully?
❏ Does the writing include confident and appropriate links and cross-references between the poems?

Sample answer

Read the sample student answer below with comments from the examiner.

Student response

'About Friends' is a poem about friendship. Brian Jones the poet makes sure that the reader knows straight away that this poem is about the goodness of friendship and how even though you haven't seen your friend in a long time, as soon as you see each other it was like you only saw each other yesterday.

The way Brian Jones structures his poem is good in my eyes because first he goes into telling us about a time two friends shared together and how they had so much fun, then he tells about when they meet up twenty years later. Things have obviously changed by then, and they were a bit cautious speaking to each other. They were adults now not kids.

My conclusion to this poem is that it is a very happy poem and the poet shows us that even though you were friends once before you still get anxious when meeting your friend after many years. It's about being sad because the river reminds him that time flows also. When reading the second poem, 'Sometimes It Happens', you get the idea that the poet Brian Patten is going over the bad things of friendship. I really like the choice of words that the poet uses. He uses simple language to show it's not always clear what happens when a friendship stops. When you think someone doesn't like you or love you it's as if the clock stops ticking.

The two poems are very different. The first one tells us that friendship is good and that friendships last forever whereas the other ('Sometimes it happens') tells us that every friend or friendship you have is doomed and is always a waste of time. In this poem there is also water flowing, but this time it stops – 'a fountain empties itself' as if it's all come to a dead end.

EXAMINER'S COMMENT

This student shows confidence when picking out details to compare the poems and digging for the big meanings. There is still more that could be said of course. The simplicity of the language perhaps makes it a little harder to quote, so it would be better to comment on the effects of phrases instead. You still do not get the feeling that the poems are being tracked systematically. You need to give a sense of a step-by-step through them to reach the highest marks.

Preparing for the exam

Here is the key information from the GCSE English Literature specification for this part of your assessment, including the Assessment Objectives related to comparing unseen poetry.

GCSE ENGLISH LITERATURE UNIT 1 Section B: poetry (contemporary)

Comparative study (14%)

Examination

For this section of the exam, you will answer **one** question comparing two contemporary unseen poems. Both poems will be printed on the question paper along with a series of bullet-point prompts to help you structure your answer.

AO1

- **Respond to texts critically and imaginatively; select and evaluate relevant textual detail to illustrate and support interpretations.**
  This means that you need to read both poems closely, and show in your answer that you are able to examine details such as the ideas covered in the poems, the writer's viewpoint and how each poet creates mood and atmosphere. You will need to support your points with quotations from the texts.

AO2

- **Explain how language, structure and form contribute to writers' presentation of ideas, themes and settings.**
  This means that you will consider how the writers use language and how they organize their poems to create particular effects on the reader. You should focus on what the language and other stylistic features add to the meaning and impact of each poem.

AO3

- **Make comparisons and explain links between texts, evaluating writers' different ways of expressing meaning and achieving effects.**
  This means that you will compare the ways in which writers use language and different techniques to express meaning and create effects. You will make links between the poems and identify similarities and differences.

Before the day

- Read as many poems as you can, especially from past exam papers. Work out how you would tackle each one in an exam.
- Get used to working with poems of different lengths.
- Practise how to begin a response; set yourself up to make sensible comments about each poem.
- Get used to using language like 'perhaps', 'possibly' and 'maybe' to show that you understand that poetry can have different meanings.
- Practise using technical language only where it helps you to make a point, avoiding empty, meaningless comments.
- Practise structuring your comparative writing; above all avoid playing ping-pong between two poems!
- Build your confidence when making personal comments in response to poems; for example, practise by offering your point of view in class discussions.

On the day

- Make sure you leave yourself a full hour for this part of the exam.
- Read with your pen in your hand, annotating the poems as you go along.
- Make sure that you read and think about both poems before you start to write your answer.
- Use the bullet points in the question on the exam paper, either as a checklist or as a structure for your response.
- Make sure you give equal attention to both poems in your writing.
- Be prepared to give 'overview' comments on both poems as well as writing about the details. These comments should look at the ideas you think the poets aim to leave you with.

Check your learning...

Having reached the end of this chapter, consider each of the points below and give yourself a rating of 1 to 4 for each one. '1' means that you still have work to do on this skill, while '4' means that you can perform this skill very well.

Can you...

- ✔ offer ideas about the voice and situation in the poems you read?
- ✔ write sensibly about two poems?
- ✔ support your points with examples and evidence from each text?
- ✔ identify similarities and differences between two poems?
- ✔ give your own personal response with some confidence?

Literary Heritage Poetry and Shakespeare

Your Assessment

In this Controlled Assessment task, you have to write about a play by Shakespeare and a selection of literary heritage poetry on the same theme. Poetry from the **literary heritage** is usually poetry that has been written in the past but is also considered to be influential or important to readers today. The chapter looks at the assignment in three parts:

1. Heritage poetry
2. Shakespeare
3. Personal response and links.

You will have **four hours** to complete your written response. Logically, the poetry writing should be completed in **one hour and 45 minutes** and the Shakespeare writing should also be completed in **one hour and 45 minutes**. The 'links' section will probably be the shortest part of the assignment, but you should set aside **at least 30 minutes** for this section.

Learn how to...

✔ write in detail about poems from the past focusing on a theme
✔ write in detail about the same theme as presented in a play by Shakespeare
✔ make personal comments about the poems and the play
✔ explore and explain connections and comparisons between the texts.

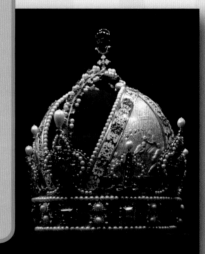

The themes

The exam board will choose two themes from the selection below each year. You will then base your linked study on one of the topics.

love

youth and age

conflict

power and ambition

family and parent-child relationships

male-female relationships and the role of women

grief

hypocrisy and prejudice

> **How does each one of the themes above affect people's lives today, in the modern world? How does each theme affect you personally?**

1.3.1 Literary Heritage Poetry

In your assignment, you will need to write in detail about literary heritage poetry in relation to one of the set themes. There are over 60 'literary heritage' poems in the poetry collection for this unit, but you will only write about a selection of them in your assignment. The more poems you read, however, the more confident you will become in your understanding of poetry in general.

> **Look at the opening lines below and on the next page. They are taken from the poetry collection for this unit. Which themes do you think might be relevant to these poems? Which poems seem to fit more than one of the themes?**

The Passionate Shepherd to His Love

Come live with me and be my love...   Christopher Marlowe

The Soldier

If I should die, think only this of me...   Rupert Brooke

On My First Son

Farewell, thou child of my right hand, and joy...   Ben Jonson

Valentine

Not a red rose or a satin heart...   Carol Ann Duffy

The Hero

'Jack fell as he'd have wished,' the Mother said...   Siegfried Sassoon

A Woman to Her Lover

Do you come to me to bend me to your will...   Christina Walsh

The Send-Off

Down the close darkening lanes they sang their way...   Wilfred Owen

---

EXAMINER'S TIP

- Be thoughtful, but be confident. If you have a hesitant idea about a poem, don't leave it in your head. If you write it down, it may get some marks, but if you don't write it down, it won't get any marks!

Unlocking the meaning of a poem

Students are often uncertain about studying poetry. They sometimes look to the teacher for the 'right' answer, but the fact is that there is generally no absolute right answer where poetry is concerned.

Bear in mind the points that follow as you read more poetry.

1. You need to build up your **confidence** with poetry. Do not worry too much about technical language. Learn to read a poem properly by reading it sentence-by-sentence.

2. You may not be able to read a poem out loud (in a Controlled Assessment, for example!) but you should try at least to **hear the words** in your head.

Look at the poem below by Siegfried Sassoon.

- **Read the poem once to yourself, sentence-by-sentence. Then, in pairs, take it in turn to read it out loud adding as much emotion to the reading as you can.**
- **What point do you think the poet is trying to make in 'Base Details'? Discuss your thoughts with your partner.**

Base Details

If I were fierce, and bald, and short of breath,
    I'd live with scarlet Majors at the Base,
And speed glum heroes up the line to death.
    You'd see me with my puffy petulant face,
5 Guzzling and gulping in the best hotel,
    Reading the Roll of Honour. 'Poor young chap,'
I'd say – 'I used to know his father well;
    Yes, we've lost heavily in this last scrap.'
And when the war is done and youth stone dead,
10 I'd toddle safely home and die – in bed.

Siegfried Sassoon

3.   Work out the **voice** (or voices) in any poem that you read. The voice refers to who is speaking in the poem and the point of view from which the poem is written. You should also try to identify the **situation** early on. The situation is **what happens** in the poem.

4.   Pay attention to the **characters** and **stories** in poems. Poems have people, places, events and twisting plots. Even the shortest poems will have a beginning, a middle and an end – in other words, they have development, moving forward rather than standing still.

Look back at 'Base Details' on the previous page and answer the questions below.

> 1.   **What do you notice about the voice in this poem? How would you describe it?**
> 2.   **What characters can you identify?**
> 3.   **What places does the poet mention and what can you say about them?**
> 4.   **How would you summarize the 'story' of the poem? It begins with the scarlet Majors at the Base but where does it end?**

5.   What kind of **mood** does the writer want to create? What are the **ideas** that the poet wishes to share? What is the **theme** and how does it develop in the content?

> **Siegfried Sassoon sets out to make a number of serious points in 'Base Details'. What ideas do you think he would like to leave the reader with?**

6.   Finally, remember not to look for a 'right answer' – there isn't one! Always be prepared to put forward **your own ideas** and opinions.

EXAMINER'S TIP

■ Different people will have different opinions about poetry and will react to it in different ways. The key is to back up your view with evidence from the text.

Use the skills above to gain an overall understanding of the poem on the next page. This poem, 'The Passionate Shepherd to His Love', was written by Christopher Marlowe in the 1500s. It is told from the point of view of a common shepherd as he asks his lover to live with him.

The Passionate Shepherd to His Love

Come live with me and be my love,
And we will all the pleasures prove
That valleys, groves, hills, and fields,
Woods, or steepy mountain yields.

5 And we will sit upon the rocks,
Seeing the shepherds feed their flocks,
By shallow rivers to whose falls
Melodious birds sing madrigals.

And I will make thee beds of roses
10 And a thousand fragrant posies,
A cap of flowers, and a kirtle
Embroidered all with leaves of myrtle.

A gown made of the finest wool
Which from our pretty lambs we pull;
15 Fair lined slippers for the cold,
With buckles of the purest gold

A belt of straw and ivy buds,
With coral clasps and amber studs;
And if these pleasures may thee move,
20 Come live with me, and be my love.

The shepherd swains shall dance and sing
For thy delight each May morning
If these delights thy mind may move,
Then live with me and be my love.

Christopher Marlowe

To understand 'The Passionate Shepherd to His Love', you should explore:

- the character of the shepherd and his voice in the poem
- the description of the landscape and lifestyle
- the possible reactions of the shepherd's loved one
- your personal response to the shepherd's feelings.

Read the poem a second time and make notes on the questions below as you read.

1. **How does the shepherd try to persuade the woman to be his love?**
2. **What kind of life does he promise her?**
3. **What is the meaning of the words 'madrigals', 'kirtle', 'myrtle', 'swains'?**
4. **Which of the five senses, such as sight and sound, does Marlowe use in this poem and what is the effect of this?**
5. **Do you think the shepherd's love would be impressed by his promises?**
6. **How realistic do you think his offer is?**

Read the following piece of writing about 'The Passionate Shepherd to His Love' written by a student. This student has tackled some of the questions above, but the answer is certainly missing something.

Student response

The shepherd asks his love to come and live with him and be his love. He describes how perfect it will be to live with nature surrounding them. He tells her what they will do together, watching the shepherds and listening to the birds singing. He also explains to her what gifts he will make for her including 'A cap of flowers' and 'A gown made of the finest wool'.

Discuss this answer with a partner. What is the biggest problem with the way the student has approached this study of the poem? What advice would you give to help the student explore the poem in more detail?

Writing about different poems

Each poem will present its own unique questions for you to investigate, but here is a set of questions you might ask yourself about any poem. You can use these questions as a basis for writing about more than one poem, but be selective and thoughtful. Choose the aspects that you can develop a little. Don't limit yourself to spotting and listing!

TOPIC	QUESTIONS TO THINK ABOUT
Themes	What particular aspect of the theme is being considered?
Viewpoint	Does the poet view the characters and emotions from a distance or is he/she 'in' the poem and experiencing them?
Mood	What kind of mood does the poet try to create? Does it change as the poem progresses?
Style	What kind of images does the poet use? Does the language include a lot of metaphors and similes? Does the poet use irony? Is the style conversational, complex, formal?
Structure	How is the poem put together? A series of arguments or a story perhaps? Is the poem separated into parts? If so, how do the parts relate to each other?
Period	When was the poem written? Do you think people may have held different attitudes then? Has the style, imagery and vocabulary of the poem been influenced by when it was written?
Personal response	Has the poet succeeded in doing what he/she set out to do? What do you find interesting about the poem?

Use the grid above to carry out an in-depth study of at least two poems that you have covered for this unit. The poems may share the same theme, but you should take time to think about how the theme is dealt with in each poem.

EXAMINER'S TIP

- Always try to make comments that show your understanding of the poem. Use technical terms only if they fit the poem that you are working on and only if you have a sensible comment to make on the features you have found.

Technical matters

You can talk about and write about poetry perfectly well without knowing many technical terms. Sometimes, technical language actually gets in the way of what you are trying to say. However, sensible use of terminology is a good thing and no one should feel it is beyond them. After all, you are meant to look at poems in detail and you need the right words to discuss what the writer is trying to do.

If a word, phrase or sentence in a poem is especially interesting or important, in your opinion, then make sure your comment deals with **how** it affects the poem's meaning.

Commenting on language choices

You will gain marks for showing that you can select and comment on particular language choices in the poems you study. When commenting on language choices, you should try to make sure that the points you make address one or a number of the questions below.

- Which words stand out as particularly important?
- Which words are especially effective or surprising?
- Do any words have underlying meanings that you find interesting?
- What images are created by descriptive vocabulary and similes or metaphors?
- How does the language involve the senses?
- Does the vocabulary create a particular mood or atmosphere?
- Does the vocabulary help to build tension in the poem?

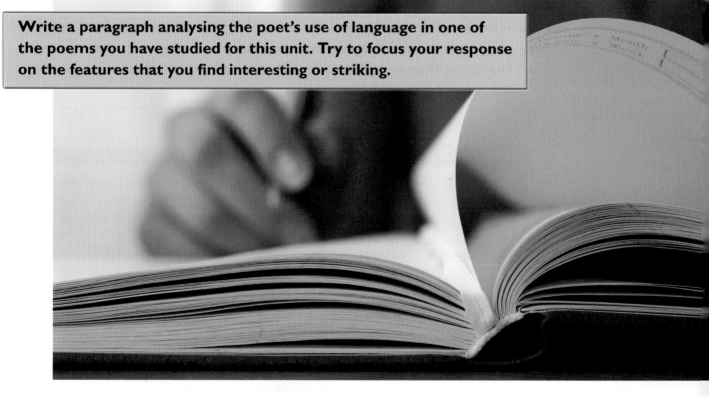

Write a paragraph analysing the poet's use of language in one of the poems you have studied for this unit. Try to focus your response on the features that you find interesting or striking.

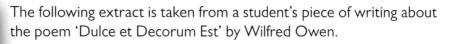

The following extract is taken from a student's piece of writing about the poem 'Dulce et Decorum Est' by Wilfred Owen.

Student response

Owen (in 'Dulce et Decorum Est') comments on blood and body parts to get the sense of pain the soldiers are going through for the country even when it is not necessary. Wilfred Owen compares the scene to cancer in the final paragraph, as cancer is awful. This poem gives the impression that the boys hate every second of the war, we can tell this from the line 'we cursed through sludge'. The word 'cursed' particularly expresses the soldier's hatred for the war.

Can you suggest ways to make this piece of writing better? How could the student write with more interest and passion?

Commenting on poetic structure

Writing about the structure of a poem need not be overly complicated. Poetic structure simply means how the poem has been put together and how it is organized on the page; features such as rhyme, line length and how the content is spread across stanzas all fall into this category.

There will often be lots of features to comment on in poems you study – but remember, you should focus on features that reveal something about what the poem **means** or **how** it achieves a particular impact on the reader.

For example, you might consider the questions below:
- Does the overall shape or structure of the poem add to your understanding?
- Are there any sound patterns worthy of comment – rhythms, rhymes or stresses?
- Does the style of language change at any points in the poem?
- Is there any use of repetition in the poem and how does this affect the overall meaning?

EXAMINER'S TIP

■ Don't make comments like, 'this poem contains lots of similes and metaphors' or 'it has an ABABCDCD rhyme scheme'. Comments like these will not help you to show your understanding of the poem. Try to comment on specific features rather than offering sweeping statements. Explain what the features reveal to you and how they add meaning and create effects.

Writing an essay on linked poetry

It is quite difficult to write an essay on poetry, so don't expect a quick solution! Here is a checklist of tips and warnings:

- Your essay needs to have a good sense of purpose from the start, so include an idea or opinion in the opening paragraph. Don't waste your first paragraph on a polite introduction.

- Make sure your essay consists of well-developed paragraphs of fairly even length, typically three to a page.

- The coverage of your chosen poems needs to be balanced. Don't set out to squeeze every last drop of detail out of every line! You'll have to give up in the end! Judge how to treat each poem in an even, balanced way – a longer poem will involve more selection of detail.

- Your essay should contain detailed references to the poems, including quotations. Quotations should be as short as possible, often a word, frequently a phrase, sometimes a sentence. Do not copy out a chunk of text to make your essay seem longer! Keep the flow of your essay going by quoting and commenting efficiently.

Don't be afraid to have ideas. Write in Standard English, but express yourself clearly, explaining what the poems mean to you.

Check your learning...

You have now reached the end of the first part of this chapter. Measure your progress by giving yourself a rating of 1 to 4 for each point below. '1' means that you still have work to do on this skill, while '4' means that you can perform this skill very well.

Can you...

- ✔ write about a poem with detailed references?
- ✔ discuss characters in poems thoughtfully?
- ✔ look more deeply into what a poem is about?
- ✔ explore the poet's language and ideas?

1.3.2 Shakespeare

As well as studying poetry for this unit, you will also study a Shakespeare play. The play will be linked to the same theme as the poetry you have studied and, like the poetry, it may deal with this theme in a number of ways.

The text you study may be a **tragedy** like *Macbeth* or *Romeo & Juliet* with a dark ending. Tragedies often end with the inevitable, fateful deaths of major characters, but even tragedies have comic moments too.

The text may be a **comedy** like *Twelfth Night* or *The Taming of the Shrew*. For most characters, Shakespearean comedies end with marriages and celebrations. Despite the lighter tone, however, comedies also have dark moments and can deal with serious issues.

Some plays, like *The Tempest* and *The Merchant of Venice*, cannot be described as either comedies or tragedies but often include features of both. These are sometimes referred to as **problem plays**.

Plays that focus on famous figures and episodes from history like *Henry V* and *Julius Caesar* are known as **history plays**.

What do you know about Shakespeare?

Read the comments from students below.

> In the time that Shakespeare lived, there was a lot of killing and you had to do what the king wanted.

> There's always a happy ending or a sad ending.

> The plays are about people and problems that are still around today.

> He wrote his plays mainly in poetry.

1. **What else do you know about Shakespeare's world?**
2. **What things do you expect to find in Shakespeare's plays?**
3. **One of the comments above mentions Shakespeare's use of poetry or 'verse' in his plays. Do you know anything else about Shakespeare's language?**
4. **Give examples of how Shakespeare is still relevant to life in the 21st century.**

Bringing the plays to life

Shakespeare's plays come to life in the theatre and on the screen. Try to be aware of how performance might affect the words on the page.

Stage directions

Stage directions are instructions included in the text for the actors performing the play. These are usually printed in italics or given in brackets in the text. Sometimes, however, the instructions are **implied** by what the actors say.

Read the extract from *Macbeth* below. In this scene Lady Macbeth waits for her husband to return, after he has gone to murder the king.

Macbeth's castle; enter Lady Macbeth

LADY MACBETH: That which hath made them drunk,
                                    hath made me bold;
                            What hath quench'd them, hath given
                                    me fire.

                    An owl shrieks

                                            Hark, peace!
                            It was the owl that shriek'd, the
                                    fatal bellman
                            Which gives the stern'st good-night.
                            He is about it.
                            The doors are open, and the surfeited grooms
                            Do mock their charge with snores. I have drugg'd their possets,
                            That death and nature do contend about them,
                            Whether they live, or die.

                    Enter Macbeth *with two bloody daggers*

MACBETH: Who's there? What ho?

What do the stage directions add to the extract?

Simply taking note of **exits** and **entrances** will help you to get a better sense of what is going on onstage.

Exits and entrances are significant because they allow you to see how characters behave differently in different situations, or when certain characters are present. The entrance of a new character may change the atmosphere; the exit of someone may cause a major rift.

- **Find an important stage direction in the play you are studying and comment on it.**
- **Find an example of an important exit or entrance in your play.**

Dramatic effects

Dramatic effects include anything which happens during a play to produce a response from members of the audience. An example is in the banquet scene in *Macbeth* when Macbeth sees the ghost of his best friend Banquo, who he arranged to have murdered. One performance of this scene is shown below. Macbeth is aware of the ghost but none of the other characters can see it.

Another example is the fight scene between the Montague and Capulet servants in the opening scene of *Romeo & Juliet*. This could be an exciting spectacle for the audience and it helps to create a visual sense of the violence that forms the background of the main plot. A photo of this scene in performance appears on page 70.

Identify a dramatic moment in the play you are studying. How is the audience likely to respond to this event? Does the event relate to any wider themes in the play?

Speech

Shakespeare's plays are made up completely of speech – but there are different forms of speech. There is speech exchanged between characters, words spoken secretively out of the hearing of others and words spoken by characters as they stand alone on stage – revealing their inner fears or dark intentions.

Conversation between characters is known as **dialogue**. This may be where characters share news with one another, argue, or make a deal.

An **aside** is a short comment made by a character that is intended to be heard by the audience, but not by anybody else onstage. A **soliloquy** is a longer speech spoken by a character who is either alone onstage or who clearly cannot be heard by other characters.

In the image opposite, Othello madly tries to come to terms with his actions, having murdered his wife. He speaks his feelings aloud though no other characters can hear him.

- **Find an example in your Shakespeare play of a character thinking aloud, so that the audience knows what he or she is thinking.**
- **Which do you think is the most important soliloquy in the Shakespeare play you are studying?**

EXAMINER'S TIP

- You don't need to learn technical terms off by heart but you should have a sense of how techniques like soliloquys and asides work. They basically give the audience an opportunity to see what a character really thinks and really feels.

Exploring themes in Shakespeare's plays

Shakespeare's plays deal with a whole range of powerful themes from friendship, to love, to relationships gone wrong, which is part of the reason why they are still relevant today! Often Shakespeare's plays deal with the same theme in a number of ways and themes may **develop** over the course of the play.

When writing about themes, you should pick out specific examples as well as showing understanding of the play as a whole. Work through the sections below to develop a detailed understanding of your play.

Know your characters

Do you know who all the characters are in the play you are studying? Do you know which characters are related? You will understand the play better if you can get these points clear in your head.

Making a note of which characters are present in each scene will also reinforce your awareness of how the characters are connected and how they interact.

Complete the following activity:

- **Create a grid like the one below. In the 'Character' column, make a list of the characters in the play you are studying in the order in which they appear.**
- **Create a column for each scene of the play. In every column, add a tick next to the characters that appear in each scene.**
- **Do you notice any patterns?**

Character	Act 1 Scene 1	Act 1 Scene 2	Act 1 Scene 3	Act 1 Scene 4	Act 1 Scene 5	Act 2 Scene 1	Act Scen

Know the plot

The **plot** is the story of the play. How would you describe what happens? How would you sum up the beginning, middle and end? Shakespeare's plots can have sudden twists, moments of suspense, and chance events that seem to have major consequences for those involved.

> ■ **Make a bullet point list of the key twists and turns of the play you are studying. Try to keep your notes short and focused.**
> ■ **What do you think is the most dramatic point in the plot?**

Spot the conflict

Some form of conflict is necessary for drama to work – even comedy. It is often the disagreement, the tension, the argument and the fighting between characters that drives the play on. The scene below is taken from a performance of *Romeo & Juliet*.

> **Summarize, in one or two sentences, the major conflict in the play you are studying. For example, is it a conflict between family members, friends or old enemies? What is the reason for the conflict?**

EXAMINER'S TIP

> ■ When you write about drama, remember to refer to the play (not the book or novel), the audience (not the reader), and the scene or act (not the chapter).

Writing an essay on Shakespeare

The play you study for this unit will obviously be much longer than any of the linked poems. You will therefore need to be **selective** in terms of what you focus on and write about. You will not be able to write about every single character and every single scene! The list below includes points to bear in mind when writing about your play.

- Don't waste your first paragraph on a long introduction. Respond to the task right from the start. The main part of your essay should consist of well-developed paragraphs of fairly even length, typically three to a page.

- Don't resort to just telling the story. When writing about a theme, you need to choose the parts of the play that best support the points that you want to make. You need to be able to nip around the play, picking out key features.

- You may decide to settle on a scene that is extra important to your case. Make sure that your writing is not too 'scattered' and deals with parts of the play in detail.

- Your essay should contain references to the text, including quotations. Quotations should be as short as possible; ideally between one word and a sentence. Avoid copying out large chunks from the play.

- Show that you are comfortable discussing the ideas that the writer is presenting. Don't be afraid to have an opinion. Write in Standard English, but express yourself clearly, explaining what the whole play and its parts mean to you.

- Make sure your final paragraph – the conclusion – avoids exact repetition of points made previously. If you can, try to add some impact to your conclusion – by making a new point or including a personal view.

Check your learning...

Now that you have reached the end of this section of the chapter, you should assess your progress against the points listed below. Give yourself a rating of 1 to 4 for each point. '1' means that you still have work to do on this skill, while '4' means that you can perform this skill very well.

Can you...

✔ write about the play with detailed references?

✔ discuss relationships in the play thoughtfully?

✔ look more deeply into what the play is about?

✔ explore Shakespeare's words and ideas?

1.3.3 Linking literary heritage poetry and Shakespeare

When you complete your final assignment for this unit, under controlled conditions, you will need to link your ideas about the poems you have studied with the Shakespeare play. The Shakespeare play and the poems will be connected by a shared theme.

The exam board will release two themes from the list below. You will write about **one** of them. The themes are:

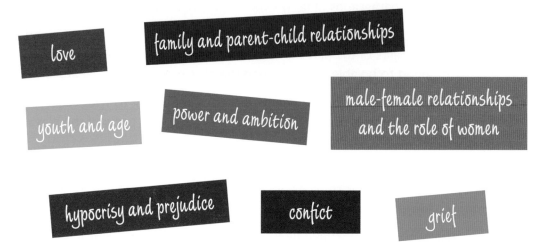

love

family and parent-child relationships

youth and age

power and ambition

male-female relationships and the role of women

hypocrisy and prejudice

conflict

grief

This chapter has encouraged you to work with the whole Shakespeare play that you are studying and a range of poems from the poetry collection. The more poems you read and the more time you spend working with your Shakespeare text, the more confident you will be when you come to write about specific sections of these texts in your final assessment.

> **EXAMINER'S TIP**
>
> ■ At first, you should aim to get to know the plot and the characters of your Shakespeare play and work out what each of the poems is about. Having read the play and the poems, you will find it easier to discuss themes and find links.

Making links

When making links between texts there are a number of topics you can think about. These topics will help you to compare the texts and identify similarities and differences between them.

The skills of the writers

This is where you look at what **techniques** the writers use to present the theme you are focusing on. What do you appreciate and admire about each of the writers? Which skills or techniques stand out as memorable?

Remember that a play, unlike the poems, is written to be performed rather than read. Do any scenes in the play appear to have a special visual quality, such as scenes of conflict or where characters express heightened emotion? Does the play make use of theatrical effects? Does it have suspense? The image on this page was taken from a performance of *The Tempest*.

Poets use carefully chosen language to create mood and atmosphere and to convey their feelings and attitudes. Do the poems have impact? Do they include language that stands out?

- **Choose two or more of the poems you have studied for this unit. For each poem, make notes on the writer's techniques Use the section above to help you.**
- **Now do the same for the play you are studying.**
- **Highlight similarities and differences.**

The ideas of the writers

While the poems and the play that you study for this unit will be linked by the same theme, the writer of each text may present the same theme differently or they may express varied ideas about it.

For each text you study, try to identify what ideas the writer is interested in. What is each writer perhaps trying to say about life, people and the world at large? Is the writer optimistic (full of hope) or pessimistic (not hopeful) about the ideas expressed in the text? What do you think the writer is trying to achieve?

- **Choose two or more of the poems you have studied for this unit. Write a paragraph about each one focusing on the ideas expressed by each writer.**
- **How are the writer's ideas similar and different in the play you have studied? Make a list of key points.**

Social, cultural and historical contexts

All of the poems that you study for this unit will have been written in the past; however, the poems may have originated from different periods in history.

For example, 'The Passionate Shepherd to His Love' by Christopher Marlowe was first published six years after the poet's death, in 1599. 'Valentine', by Carol Ann Duffy, was first published in 1993. Both poems deal with the theme of love – but each writer takes a different approach to the topic. This subject-matter is influenced by the time period in which each poem was written.

> **How else do you think historical context might have influenced 'The Passionate Shepherd to His Love' and 'Valentine'? How might it have influenced each poet's attitude to the theme of love?**

In addition to differences, you may also find similarities where you least expect them. Shakespeare wrote most of his plays between the end of the 16th century and the beginning of the 17th century. Despite this, many of his characters and the themes he deals with still seem very relevant to life today.

> ■ **Think about the play you are studying. What does the play reveal about the attitudes of the past?**
> ■ **In what ways are the characters timeless, showing unchanging human characteristics?**

Your personal response

Another way to link your study of the poems to the study of your Shakespeare play is to consider your **personal response** to the texts. Have you learned anything from the texts? If so, what have you learned? Has the play or any of the poems changed your opinions in any way?

> **Write down your personal reponse to some of the texts you have sudied for this unit. Use the section above to help you. Do not settle for short answers – develop your thoughts.**

Controlled Assessment practice

The following sample task is based on a study of *Romeo & Juliet* and the poem 'Valentine' by Carol Ann Duffy. The student response is presented in three parts – one section for each bullet point. Read the response and examiner's comments that follow.

- Examine the way Shakespeare presents the beginning of the relationship between Romeo and Juliet in the early part of the play. In your response, make references to other parts of the play.
- Examine how the theme of love is presented in poems from the poetry collection.
- What is your response to the pieces of literature you have read? Make links between the ways the writers have considered and presented the theme.

- Examine the way Shakespeare presents the beginning of the relationship between Romeo and Juliet in the early part of the play. In your response, make references to other parts of the play.

Student response part 1

In the beginning of the play, Romeo & Juliet by Shakespeare, we are told of the warring families, 'The Capulets' and 'The Montagues'. There is no explanation of why they fight but it is all part of the story and the key reason why the story develops as it does.

Romeo is introduced to us as a lovesick man, who is in love with Rosaline, he is shown as a character that spends time on his own, and his friends are unsure of how to deal with him when he talks about his love.

The prologue tells us what will happen before we read the play and understand the characters, 'A pair of star-cross'd lovers take their life.' The Capulet family are planning for Juliet to be married to Paris and you see her mother and Nurse discussing that she is very young but it is the right age when she is only fourteen. Juliet is shown at this time in Act 1 Scene 3 to be an obedient young lady wanting to please her family and when asked about marriage she replies, 'It is an honour that I dream not of'.

Romeo sees Juliet for the first time when he and his friends gatecrash the Capulet's ball, wearing masks so they will not be recognized as the enemy. When he sees Juliet he falls in love at first sight:

What lady's that which doth enrich the hand/Of yonder knight?

He is attracted to Juliet straight away and thinks she is the most beautiful lady he has even seen, forgetting about Rosaline immediately, declaring 'Did my heart love till now?'

Within a few minutes of meeting each other, Romeo has kissed Juliet. Shakespeare moves the pace along very quickly and it is clear that the two are completely in love. It is only after the kisses that Juliet's nurse tells Romeo who Juliet is, which shocks him: 'Is she a Capulet? O dear account! My life is my foe's debt.' He leaves hurriedly. Juliet is heartbroken when she realizes he is a part of her family's enemy: 'My only love sprung from my only hate!'

The lovers have met and realized how dangerous their love is, but this is only the beginning and they do not forget about each other. Romeo goes to Capulet's house and they meet once again. The scene that follows shows them expressing their love and they plan to be married regardless of their families. This can only spell trouble and the lines in Act 2 Scene 2, Juliet saying: 'And all my fortunes at thy foot I'll lay, And follow thee my lord throughout the world', are a sad indication of what is to come.

Their relationship is never going to work and they have two people that agree to help them be married, the nurse and Friar Lawrence. Both of these characters assist them and yet play a key role in the deaths of the lovers. By agreeing to marry them, the Friar seals their fate. It is after the secret marriage that the fighting begins in seriousness and characters from both families die. The secrecy also leads to the confusion that brings about the death of the lovers themselves. Juliet plans to take a sleeping potion to let everyone believe she has died and to avoid marrying Paris.

Sadly it backfires, as Romeo finds Juliet and believing her to be really dead takes his own poison and dies, before she awakens and kills herself to be with him. It is a sad story that could have been so different.

EXAMINER'S COMMENT

This is a very bright personal response from someone who has clearly engaged with the play. It perhaps would benefit a little from less re-telling of the plot and more focus on particular scenes and dialogue with detailed examples. However, the kind of confident discussion that is shown here is very pleasing and should be encouraged in any answer.

- *Examine how the theme of love is presented in poems from the poetry collection.*

Student response part 2

In the poem 'Valentine' by Carol Ann Duffy, Duffy's ideas of love are quite different to most people, it isn't the traditional view of love with hearts and roses and chocolates. The fact that she uses an onion indicates her unusual ideas. The onion represents 'love' to her. She believes that lovers give you grief a lot of the time like onions make you cry. She also believes that true love will stay with you forever like the smell of an onion will cling to you. This reminds me of how Shakespeare describes love as an 'ever-fixed mark' in 'Sonnet 116'.

Duffy also suggests that the loops of an onion after cutting it, represent a wedding ring; she believes that marriage is something to be cautious of as it can spoil love which is an interesting idea. The phrase 'wrapped in brown paper' is a metaphor for hidden things, parcels which are eagerly waited for, people look forward to falling in love and think it will be like a parcel.

I think the word 'truthful' summarizes the whole of Duffy's poem, it is the real truth about love not the traditional one represented by hearts and roses. Duffy believes love isn't all about pleasant things. This is quite different to 'The Passionate Shepherd to His Love' by Christopher Marlow, for example, where the shepherd thinks that life with his love will be perfect. Duffy relates love to mixed emotions and feelings, it can be clingy and love has its good and bad points.

When Duffy says 'fierce kiss' it makes you think, as kisses are supposed to be gentle and kind, not fierce. Being possessive can also not be good thing, Duffy has an unusual but more realistic view on love in this poem.

EXAMINER'S COMMENT

Again, with the poem, the student shows free and fluent understanding though there is a clear need for a more methodical tracking of the poem from start to finish. Equally, it does seem a shame that a response to a second poem is not developed, for it would seem that the student is very capable of handling comparisons and links in this area.

- What is your response to the pieces of literature you have read? Make links between the ways the writers have considered and presented the theme.

Student response part 3

The pieces I have read are all about love, but Duffy's 'Valentine' and Shakespeare's play both show how love can be 'lethal'. Romeo and Juliet is a play that is filled with sadness that two young lovers cannot be together because of their families and the hatred that has been built up; it also moves very quickly and shows the darker side of love.

Duffy's poem 'Valentine' does the same as it is not all happiness and roses. She shows that love can be cruel and 'it will blind you with tears', the same as Romeo & Juliet where there seems to be a lot of heartbreak and crying, particularly from Juliet who is heartbroken when she learns that Romeo is a Montague and then when she believes him to be dead.

Duffy talks about how a 'fierce kiss will stay on your lips', which is a strange idea about kissing, when it is meant to be kind and loving. In Romeo & Juliet the two lovers both drink potions, Romeo kills himself with poison and ironically Juliet kisses him to get some of the poison onto her lips before putting a dagger in her heart. So both pieces are linked by this idea of kissing being a bad thing.

Both Duffy's poem and Shakespeare's play show how it is not easy to be in love and the unhappiness that it can bring. Duffy says 'cling to your knife' again linked to how Juliet kills herself and although Duffy is meaning that love will cling to you, it is taken in the opposite way in Romeo and Juliet.

Romeo and Juliet is a story of love and how it affects two people in a way that is 'lethal' when Duffy uses the word 'lethal' it is for impact not in the way that the story ends with Shakespeare.

I find Duffy's poem 'Valentine' interesting as a different view to the whole idea of love being wonderful. It is opposite to poems like 'A Passionate Shepherd to His Love' and 'Sonnet 116'. I think it is more realistic. Romeo & Juliet also shows the darker side of love as it tells a sad story, where both lovers kill themselves because they cannot be together.

EXAMINER'S COMMENT

The assignment is completed strongly with a thoughtful and fairly well-sustained third and final part. The student is comfortable with the technique of comparing and appears to have no problem seeing links and writing them down. The third part of the three-part assignment is generally expected to be the shortest section of the response, but in this case the student has recovered lost ground with a longer contribution, including more links and more detail.

How is the linked essay on Shakespeare and poetry assessed at GCSE?

Use the checklist below to assess your progress and see where you could make improvements.

Reading and understanding texts: is there…

- ❏ a reasonable attempt to respond to both the play and some of the poems – pointing out some basic links?
- ❏ a detailed response to both the play and the poems, with personal opinions given and cross-references between texts?
- ❏ a clear understanding of the relevant theme as covered in both the play and the poems?
- ❏ an in-depth understanding of the relevant theme as covered in both the play and the poems?

Writer's ideas: is there…

- ❏ some response to characters, relationships and main events?
- ❏ some use of evidence from the text to back up points?
- ❏ evidence of relevant personal views about the text supported by well-chosen references to language and structure?
- ❏ a confident exploration of characters and ideas, supported by reference to how language and structure is used to create meaning?

Expression and organization: does your essay show…

- ❏ coverage of both texts in relation to the theme with a personal response used to link texts?
- ❏ a response that covers all parts of the task?
- ❏ a focused response that is relevant to the question and theme throughout?
- ❏ a focused response that provides a detailed exploration of how different writers deal with the same theme?

Preparing for Controlled Assessment

Here is the key information from the GCSE specification for this part of your assessment, including the Assessment Objectives related to the linked essay.

GCSE ENGLISH LITERATURE UNIT 3: Poetry and drama

Literary heritage poetry and Shakespeare play (25% of final GCSE mark)

Controlled Assessment

For this assessment, you will need to write a response to **one** task linking the study of a play by Shakespeare to a range of literary heritage poems. The poems will be chosen from a poetry collection supplied by your exam board.

AO1

- **Respond to texts critically and imaginatively; select and evaluate relevant textual detail to illustrate and support interpretations.**
  This means that you need to read both the Shakespeare play and the poems closely, and show in your writing that you are able to explore the subject-matter and ideas and themes covered in each text. You will need to support your points by selecting relevant details and quotations from the texts.

AO2

- **Explain how language, structure and form contribute to writers' presentation of ideas, themes and settings.**
  This means that you will consider how the writers use language to create effects when dealing with a particular theme. You will also write about how pieces of writing are organized and the effects of this.

AO3

- **Make comparisons and explain links between texts, evaluating writers' different ways of expressing meaning and achieving effects.**
  This means that you will compare the ways in which writers deal with a particular theme using language and different techniques to present the theme to the reader or audience. You will make links between the texts and identify similarities and differences.

GCSE ENGLISH UNIT 3: English in the world of the imagination

Reading: literary heritage poetry and Shakespeare play (10% of final GCSE mark)

Controlled Assessment

For this assessment, you will need to write a response to **one** task linking the study of a play by Shakespeare to a range of literary heritage poems. The poems will be chosen from a poetry collection supplied by your exam board.

AO2 Reading

- **Read and understand texts, selecting material appropriate to purpose, collating from different sources and making comparisons and cross-references as appropriate.**

  This means that you need to read both the Shakespeare play and the poems closely, identifying similarities and differences between them. You will need to select relevant evidence and quotations from the texts to support your points.

- **Develop and sustain interpretations of writers' ideas and perspectives.**

  This means that you must show in your writing that you are able to explore the subject-matter and ideas and themes covered in each text.

- **Explain and evaluate how writers use linguistic, grammatical, structural and presentational features to achieve effects and engage and influence the reader.**

  This means that you will consider how the writers use language to create effects when dealing with a particular theme. You will also write about how pieces of writing are organized and the effects of this.

- **Understand texts in their social, cultural and historical contexts.**

  This means that you will suggest how the social, cultural or historical background of a text might affect the way the writer deals with the theme you are focusing on. This might include factors such as when a text was written, who wrote it and what the writer was hoping to achieve.

Writing your assignment

Will I have time in class to prepare my essay?

Yes, after you have studied the play and the poems in class, you will have up to 15 hours of lesson time to make notes on your texts and plan your approach to the task. You will be able to study your texts in detail and discuss the texts and the theme with other students.

Can I have help from the teacher?

Your teacher can help you in the normal way – by teaching the class and talking to you individually. However, you are not allowed to obtain help from your teacher during your revision.

How long is the Controlled Assessment?

For the linked essay, the time allowed for the final stage of the Controlled Assessment is **four hours**. This is where you will write your response. The time allowed will probably be broken down into shorter sessions and your teacher will collect in your work at the end of each session. You will not be able to work on your response outside these sessions, and once you have handed in your work at the end of the last session, you will not be able to amend it.

Can I take the play and the poems into the Controlled Assessment with me?

In the final assessment you will have access to a copy of your Shakespeare text and the full collection of poems for this unit. The texts must be **clean copies**, which means that they must not have any notes in them. You will, however, be allowed to take in one A4 sheet of **your own** notes to refer to as you write your final answer.

How will my linked essay be marked?

Your work on the play and the poems will be marked by your teacher. It will be marked out of 40 as one complete essay.

Check your learning...

Now that you have reached the end of this chapter, look at the points below and assess your progress. Give yourself a rating of 1 to 4 for each point. 'I' means that you still have work to do on this skill, while '4' means that you can perform this skill very well.

Can you...

✔   explore the treatment of a particular theme in the poems and play that you have studied?

✔   compare and judge the subject-matter, purpose, tone and impact of the texts?

✔   make personal comments about the poems and the play?

✔   explore and explain connections and comparisons between texts?

Your Assessment

This chapter deals with the skills you need to write an essay on a long text. All <u>examples</u> in this unit relate to different cultures novels. All <u>skills</u> covered in this unit relate closely to the skills covered in Chapter 1.3 and Chapter 1.4.

If you are studying **GCSE English**, you will have to write an essay on a different cultures novel. You will study **one** of five texts set by the exam board and will complete your essay in a Controlled Assessment.

If you are studying **GCSE English Language**, you have to write an essay on an extended literary text, which <u>could be</u> a different cultures novel. You might, however, study another prose text or play, which your teacher will choose from a list set by the exam board. You will complete your essay in a Controlled Assessment.

Learn how to...

- ✔ write about a long text in detail and as a whole
- ✔ make valid points about characters and themes in the text
- ✔ show that you understand the relevant contexts
- ✔ give a personal response to the text and build this into your writing.

Can you write about the detail of your text?

Do you know the text you are studying well enough to write in some detail about it? In your assessment you will need to select details from the text and comment on them in response to your task. This might mean referring to particular events in the plot or things the characters say and do. You should also be able to back up your points with short quotations and write about the effects of the language.

> **Read the student response on *Of Mice and Men* below and comment on the different ways the student uses details from the book.**

Student response

In the part of the novel where Candy's dog is killed you can tell straight away that Candy doesn't want it to be shot. This is shown when Candy tries to put it off 'Maybe to-morra'. Candy looks at Slim to get some help because he knows he is going to be out voted. Candy says 'Awight take him' He says 'hopelessly' and 'softly'. You can tell that Candy and his dog are very close as when Carlson takes the dog Candy can't even look at him. Candy rolls over waiting to hear the shot. A lot of tension is built as it is silent; Candy is waiting anxiously for the gun shot. There is a comparison between this scene and the end scene as Lennie gets shot the way Candy's dog does. There is also a comparison between Candy and Lennie. Lennie is mentally disabled and Candy and his dog are both physically disabled.

EXAMINER'S TIP

■ When writing about the detail of a long text it is important to be **selective**. Pick the details that are most relevant to your task and only include them where you have something specific to say.

Can you write about the text as a whole?

Do you know the text well enough to write about it as a whole? This is where you might identify themes that run throughout the text or link different parts of it together to make points about its wider meaning. You might notice parallels between characters for example, or events that appear to be related to a similar cause.

> **Read the second response on *Of Mice and Men* below. Comment on any strengths and weaknesses you can spot in this piece of writing.**

Student response

Candy's dog is his one and only friend; he had him since he was a puppy. But his dog is taken away from him, he becomes like the other men, he has no-one else.

Of Mice and Men is harsh because no one achieves their dreams. Lennie does, he's the only one, but he only achieves it because George helps him to. George doesn't achieve it and never will, he only thought he could achieve it because of Lennie but now Lennie is gone.

I believe Of Mice and Men is a world of harshness and violence because of its loneliness and the lack of achievement. John Steinbeck shows us how tough life is, and how difficult it is to escape poverty.

EXAMINER'S TIP

- You will be expected to show some awareness and understanding of the time and place in which your text is set. However, you should only include details about this background to the text where it links to your task and the precise point you want to make. Remember this is an English assessment, not a history one!

What makes 'different cultures' different?

The world is made up of people from all kinds of different backgrounds and communities, speaking and writing in different languages and passing on the memories and experiences that have been important to people for centuries.

Literature from different cultures allows us to see how the wider world works. As novels tend to deal with people and the challenges they face, novels from different cultures let us see how people are affected in various places throughout the world, not all of them far from home.

Does it make any difference where and when a story takes place? Discuss your opinions with a partner.

The extract below is taken from *Chanda's Secrets* by Allan Stratton. The novel focuses on 16-year-old Chanda Kabelo and the struggles that she and her family face. The novel is set in a fictional part of southern Africa.

Chanda's Secrets

Home wasn't always a shantytown in Bonang.

Our family started out on Papa's cattle post, a spread of grazing land near the village of Tiro, about two hundred miles north. I shared a one-room mud hut with Mama, Papa, an older sister and three older brothers. (There would have been two other sisters, but they died before I was born. One from bad water, one from gangrene)...

...Life on the cattle post was slow. In winter, the riverbeds dried up and the sparrows' nests hung like straw apples from the acacia trees. All the plants shrivelled to the bare ground, and only the mopane trees and a few jackalberries kept us from being desert. Me and my cousins would spend the days helping our mamas collect well water, or herding the cattle with our papas.

Why do you think the setting is important in this novel? How might understanding the setting help you to better appreciate the issues faced by the characters?

When you study your chosen text, you will look at how it presents a particular way of life and how this reflects or influences the way you think about your own life. You may discover situations that seem unfamiliar. However, you are also likely to recognize similarities in the hopes and dreams shared by people around the world.

In 'different cultures' texts you might:
- witness a world of harshness and struggle
- be shocked by prejudice and injustice
- admire how people cope with racism
- marvel how people stand up to loss and tragedy
- perhaps even smile at someone caught between two cultures.

> **Think about the text you are studying. Does it feature any of the points listed above? Give details for each one.**

Openings

The beginning of a novel will often try to capture the reader's attention. The writer may plunge the reader straight into the action, or start by setting the scene – giving hints about what is to come.

When looking at openings, think about the following questions:
- How does the story start?
- What is the first paragraph or page made up of?
- How are you drawn into the story?
- What holds your attention?
- How much does the writer tell you?
- Is it possible to tell how the story will develop?

> **Look at the opening section of your text and note down some ideas for each question above. Do not settle for short answers – develop your thoughts.**

EXAMINER'S TIP

- Endings are of course just as worthy of your close attention. How has the writer decided to end the narrative? What messages do you think the writer is trying to leave you with? From a practical point of view make sure you know what has happened to all the major characters by the end of the novel.

Writing about characters

Different people are likely to have different opinions about characters. You may find that you are puzzled by what a character does or you may feel that you would act in a similar way if you found yourself in the same situation as them.

> **Read the passage from *Of Mice and Men* below. What are your thoughts and feelings about what happens in this extract?**

Of Mice and Men

Lennie dabbled his big paw in the water and wiggled his fingers so the water arose in little splashes; rings widened across the pool to the other side and came back again. Lennie watched them go. "Look, George. Look what I done."

George knelt beside the pool and drank from his hand with quick scoops. "Tastes all right," he admitted. "Don't really seem to be running, though. You never oughta drink water when it ain't running, Lennie," he said hopelessly. "You'd drink out of a gutter if you was thirsty." He threw a scoop of water into his face and rubbed it about with his hand, under his chin and around the back of his neck. Then he replaced his hat, pushed himself back from the river, drew up his knees, and embraced them. Lennie, who had been watching, imitated George exactly. He pushed himself back, drew up his knees, embraced them, looked over to George to see whether he had it just right. He pulled his hat down a little more over his eyes, the way George's hat was.

> **Choose a moment from the text you are studying that reveals something about a character. With detailed reference to the text, write down your thoughts and feelings towards the character.**

When writing about characters, you should try to think about how particular characters are important to the text as a whole. Who are the main characters of the story? What strikes you about them? Are there interesting conflicts and relationships between the characters?

You should try to think about the results of a character's actions on the main plot and also the subplots of the story. Does the character develop or change during the story and, if so, how?

> **Choose a key character from your text. What do you think is the importance of this character to the story as a whole? Put together a plan including five ideas.**
> **Try to include:**
> ■ **main ideas about the character**
> ■ **detailed evidence from the text.**

EXAMINER'S TIP

■ When writing about a character, think about how the character is presented to the reader. Think about the writer's use of description, dialogue and actions and also the reactions of other characters.

Writing about themes

A **theme** in literature is an idea or topic that a writer wishes to develop or repeat through the characters and action of the novel or play. The theme will be brought to life by the way the characters behave and the way the story progresses.

The extract on the next page is from *Anita & Me* by Meera Syal, and captures a moment where the main character's mother attempts to explain what the festival of Diwali is to a neighbour. The novel is set in a small village near Wolverhampton in the 1970s.

Anita & Me

Mama had been cooking and cleaning for weeks it seemed because today was Diwali – 'Our Christmas, Mrs Worrall,' mama had told her, not wanting to go into huge detail about the Hindu Festival of Light and why the date changed each year, being a lunar festival, and how we did not give presents but put on all the lights in the house and gambled instead to welcome the goddess Lakshmi into our lives, hoping she would bring luck and wealth with her. Christmas was not the best comparison to use in front of me because I naturally expected a carload of presents and the generally festive, communal atmosphere that overtook the village somewhere around late November and continued into January.

But no one else in the world seemed to care that today was our Christmas. There was no holiday, except it happened to be a weekend…

What themes does the writer deal with in this extract? What can you say about each theme?

The reader will often be left to work out the messages coming from the novel. Different themes will be intertwined and some will be harder to spot than others. Revenge, loneliness, childhood, prejudice are just a few of the more obvious themes that you may meet and be required to discuss in your study of the text.

When writing about themes remember to consider:
- what the characters' speech and actions reveal about the theme
- different events in the plot and how they influence the theme.

> **Choose an important theme from your text. How does the writer present this theme? Put together an essay plan in response to this question.**

Giving a personal response

In many ways, every comment you make on a text – providing it represents your own ideas – is part of your personal response. Giving a good personal response is a matter of being confident about your opinions and being thoughtful in your writing.

The list below includes questions to help you to develop your own personal opinions as you study your text:
- What do you appreciate and admire about the way the writer has written the story?
- Have you learned anything from the book?
- Has it changed (or perhaps confirmed) your opinions in any way?
- How did you feel reading the book and, now, having read it?
- What is your attitude to the writer after reading the story?

> **Discuss the text you are studying with a group of at least two other students. Take it in turns to put your view forward in response to each of the questions above.**

EXAMINER'S TIP

■ A personal response is more than just saying, 'I really liked this book', or, 'Slim is my favourite character'; it is about making intelligent points about the effects the text has on you as a reader and **how** it manages to achieve this. You need to back up your reasons with direct references to the text.

Humour

Different people are certain to have different opinions about what they find funny or amusing about texts. However, unfamiliar situations do produce comic scenes and moments that make you smile or even laugh out loud. Sometimes, you might find yourself laughing at the character and sometimes you might be laughing with them.

In the extract from *To Kill a Mockingbird* below, the main character, Scout, describes her first day at school. She is taught by a young teacher who is new to the area.

> **What is amusing about the way the narrator describes the situation? What messages do you think the humour helps to put across?**

To Kill a Mockingbird

Miss Caroline began the day by reading us a story about cats. The cats had long conversations with one another, they wore cunning little clothes and lived in a warm house beneath a kitchen stove. By the time Mrs Cat called the drugstore for an order of chocolate malted mice the class was wriggling like a bucketful of catawba worms. Miss Caroline seemed unaware that the ragged, denim-shirted and floursack-skirted first grade, most of whom had chopped cotton and fed hogs from the time they were able to walk, were immune to imaginative literature. Miss Caroline came to the end of the story and said, '*Oh*, my, wasn't that nice?'

Then she went to the blackboard and printed the alphabet in enormous square capitals, turned to the class and asked, 'Does anybody know what these are?'

Everybody did; most of the first grade had failed it last year.

> **Choose an extract from the novel that you are studying where the writer uses humour. Explain how the humour works.**

Mood and atmosphere

As well as having characters, events and theme, novels also have a particular mood or atmosphere. This mood and atmosphere is likely to change as the story progresses to reflect the action and events in the plot. There may be tense moments of suspense, where a character seems to balance on the edge of disaster; there may be moments of joy and celebration; there may also be moments where the narrator seems quite detached from the events he or she describes.

The best way to detect and describe a particular mood or atmosphere is to describe how the text makes you feel, and then work out what techniques the writer is using to make you feel this way.

Read the extract below from *I Know Why the Caged Bird Sings* by Maya Angelou. The book tells the story of the author's life, growing up as a black woman in America in the 1930s. In this extract she watches as a group of white school girls make fun of her grandmother.

I Know Why the Caged Bird Sings

Before the girls got to the porch I heard their laughter crackling and popping like pine logs in a cooking stove. I suppose my lifelong paranoia was born in those cold, molasses-slow minutes. They came finally to stand on the ground in front of Momma. At first they pretended seriousness. Then one of them wrapped her right arm in the crook of her left, pushed out her mouth and started to hum. I realized that she was aping my grandmother. Another said, "Naw, Helen, you ain't standing like her. This here's it…"

…Through the fly-specked screen-door, I could see the arms of Momma's apron jiggled from the vibrations of her humming. But her knees seemed to have locked as if they would never bend again. She sang on. No louder than before, but no softer either. No slower or faster.

As you study your text, try to be aware of shifts in the mood and atmosphere. What is the mood and atmosphere like at the start of the story and how is the reader likely to react to this? How does this change, if at all, as the story progresses?

> **How would you describe the mood and atmosphere in the extract?**
> **How does the writer create this effect?**

Feelings

Most novels will contain one or more characters who the reader is likely to sympathize with. If you 'sympathize' with a character, it basically means that you are able to see things from the character's point of view. It means you see why the character feels and acts in a certain way and that you appreciate his or her situation.

In the extract below from *Of Mice and Men*, George defends Lennie for his part in a fight with Curley, in which Curley's hand is badly crushed.

Of Mice and Men

George broke in, "Lennie was jus' scairt," he explained. "He didn't know what to do. I told you nobody ought never to fight him. No, I guess it was Candy I told."

Candy nodded solemnly. "That's jus' what you done," he said. "Right this morning when Curley first lit intil your fren', you says, 'He better not fool with Lennie if he knows what's good for 'um.' That's jus' what you says to me."

George turned to Lennie. "It ain't your fault," he said. "You don't need to be scairt no more. You done jus' what I tol' you to. Maybe you better go in the wash room an' clean up your face. You look like hell."

Lennie smiled with his bruised mouth. "I didn't want no trouble," he said. He walked toward the door, but just before he came to it, he turned back.

"George?"

"What you want?"

"I can still tend to the rabbits, George?"

"Sure. You ain't done nothing wrong."

"I di'nt mean no harm, George."

"Well, get the hell out and wash your face."

> **Which character do you sympathize with most in the extract and why? Discuss your opinions with a partner.**

Writing a Controlled Assessment essay on a long text

It is quite difficult to write an essay on a long text, so don't expect a quick solution! Here is a checklist of tips and warnings.

- You need to aim for an essay of approximately **three to five sides of A4 paper** (average-sized handwriting). Anything much less than three sides is unlikely to be detailed enough.

- Your essay needs a good sense of **purpose** from the outset, so get an idea or opinion in the opening paragraph. Tackle the task right from the start.

- Make sure your essay consists of **well-developed paragraphs** of fairly even length, typically three to a page. Make sure your final paragraph – the conclusion – avoids exact repetition of points you have already made.

- The coverage of a long text has to be **highly selective**. Don't resort to just telling the story. If you are writing about a theme or a character, you need to choose the parts of the text that best support the points that you want to make.

- You may decide to settle on **one or two parts of the text** that are especially relevant to your task. Is there a part of your essay that perhaps concentrates on one incident from the text and explores it?

- Your essay should contain **detailed references** to the text, including quotations. Quotations should be as short as possible. Do not copy out a chunk of text to make your essay seem longer! Keep the flow of your essay going by quoting and commenting efficiently.

- Show that you are comfortable discussing the **ideas and themes** that the writer is presenting. Don't be afraid to have ideas. Write in **Standard English**, but express yourself clearly, trying to explain what the whole text and its parts mean to you.

Controlled Assessment practice

If you are studying a different cultures prose text or another play or novel for a Controlled Assessment, you will know what the task is well before you write your final response. This means that you will have time to think about it and develop your ideas in lessons.

The example task below is based on *I Know Why the Caged Bird Sings* by Maya Angelou.

> Write about the relationship between Maya and Bailey Junior as they grow up, and how it changes and develops.

Student response

Maya and Bailey Junior's relationship develops and grows throughout the book. However, some things stay the same like the love they feel for each other – even if it is tested at some points.

From a young age Bailey and Maya have had to depend on each other for comfort and for someone to talk to in their time of need, they try to do most things together like learning and playing. Maya describes how they 'rattle off the times tables' together and go over what they learnt. We also learn that they grieve and cry together and share the same emotions – 'and nights we had cried together', which suggests their closeness. Twins often feel each other's pain or discomfort because they are so closely matched; in some ways I think Bailey and Maya could be compared to twins as their feelings for each other are so strong. In Stamps they do most things together, 'Bailey and I' is a phrase used a lot in the beginning of the novel which indicates that they're pretty much inseparable.

However, when they meet their parents their feelings for each other change and Maya feels like she's being replaced as Bailey's companion and close friend. Near the beginning of the novel, Maya informs us that Bailey was 'my only brother' and that she had 'no sisters to share with him'. We can also tell that she really admires and adores Bailey and she's so lucky that he 'loves' her even though she's the complete contrast to him and feels that she's 'ugly'. Therefore when her parents enter the picture, Maya surely feels that the relationship is at risk.

This results in Maya not liking her parents and not really making any efforts to get on well with them. After her father arrives she says that her 'seven-year-old world humpty-dumptied, never to be put back together again', which tells us how uncertain she feels about meeting them. When she meets her mother she feels over-powered by jealousy because she says 'they were more alike than he and I' which indicates that she feels deserted by Bailey because he's giving attention to his mother. This really tested their relationship to the limit because Maya felt betrayed.

The incident with Mr Freeman also affects their relationship greatly. This is the first secret Maya had 'ever kept from Bailey'. This indicates that Maya's beginning to feel isolated and feels like she's growing apart from Bailey. However, she does hope that he would 'read it on my face' but sadly Bailey doesn't, which reinforces the fact that Maya feels alienated.

We also find out that before Mr Freeman attacks Maya, Bailey and her go out but to different places – her to the 'library' and he goes to 'play baseball'. This is a clear contrast to when they were in Stamps when they used to do a lot together. This also tells us that Bailey wasn't protecting Maya from Mr Freeman as he was out busy playing with his friends – this shows that they are growing apart.

However, after the family find out about the rape, Bailey tells Maya that there's no danger of him getting hurt and that he'll fight anyone who did this, and their relationship becomes as solid as a rock once more. We also find that when Mr Freeman threatens Maya she stays faithful to Bailey because she doesn't tell a soul. This suggests that their relationship is very strong and withstands everything.

EXAMINER'S COMMENT

The student here provides a genuine discussion in response to a task that is not actually set in question form, but which requires focus on the changing and developing relationship of Maya and Bailey Junior. There is a good sense of balance in this essay, with a clear range of well-chosen incidents and 'chapters' covered. This student has been very effective in selecting material from the text and the points are clear, well explained and well linked.

How is the essay on a long text assessed at GCSE?

Use the questions below to check your performance when writing an essay on an extended text, such as a different cultures prose text.

Does the response to the text...
❑ show some personal response to the text and general knowledge of the story?
❑ show some selection of relevant detail to support points?
❑ discuss characters and relationships thoughtfully?
❑ discuss wider themes in the text and provide examples?
❑ deal confidently with the whole text, with an overview and ability to move from the specific to the general?

Are there...
❑ simple comments about language choices?
❑ simple comments on particular features of style and structure?
❑ comments about how different aspects of style and structure help to create effects, meanings and ideas?
❑ developed comments on language, structure and form exploring meaning and effects?

Is there...
❑ a selection of simple comments on the background of the text?
❑ a clear grasp of the relevant social, cultural and historical contexts?
❑ some consideration of the importance of social, cultural and historical contexts when reading and responding to the text?
❑ a selection of evidence from the text, which is used to support an overall understanding of the relevant social, cultural and historical contexts?

Is the expression (the grammar, punctuation and spelling)...
❑ likely to make the response unclear in places?
❑ reasonably clear with a good basic sense of structure?
❑ mainly clear with only minor errors?
❑ clear and fluent, with few errors in grammar, punctuation and spelling?

Preparing for Controlled Assessment

Here is a breakdown of the key information from the GCSE English and GCSE English Language specifications for writing an essay on an extended text. This section includes the Assessment Objectives for each assessment, which show you how your work will be marked.

GCSE ENGLISH UNIT 3: English in the world of the imagination (reading)

Different cultures prose (10%)

Controlled Assessment

For this part of your assessment, you will complete **one** task on one different cultures prose text. You will have time to study your text and develop your ideas in response to the task in lesson time. However, you will have **two hours** to complete your final written response. You should aim to write 800-1000 words.

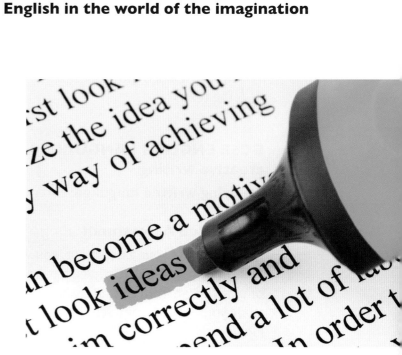

You will be allowed to take a copy of the text into the assessment with you providing you have not made any notes in it. You will, however, be allowed to prepare one A4 sheet of your own notes before the assessment and refer to these notes as you write your final answer.

AO2 Reading

- **Read and understand texts, selecting material appropriate to purpose, collating from different sources and making comparisons and cross-references as appropriate.**
  For this part of the assessment, this means that you need to read the whole text and be able to select details from it to support the points you want to make. Making links between different parts of the novel will also help you to put together a stronger answer.

- **Develop and sustain interpretations of writers' ideas and perspectives.**
  As well as being able to write about the novel in detail, you also need to get a sound overview of it. This means that you should be comfortable writing about themes in the text and the ideas and opinions expressed by the writer.

- **Explain and evaluate how writers use linguistic, grammatical, structural and presentational features to achieve effects and engage and influence the reader.**

  This means that you will consider how the writer uses language and stylistic features to create particular effects on the reader. You will also write about how events are structured in the novel and how this structure also works to create meaning.

- **Understand texts in their social, cultural and historical contexts.**

  This point relates to the background of the novel. Do you know when and where it is set? How does this influence the way you read and respond to the text?

GCSE ENGLISH LANGUAGE UNIT 3: Literary reading and creative writing

Studying written language: Extended literary text (15%)

Controlled Assessment

For this part of your assessment, you will complete **one** task on one extended text. This <u>may be</u> a different cultures prose text or it could be another prose text or play chosen from a list of texts set by the exam board. You will have time to study your text and develop your ideas in response to the task in lesson time. However, you will have **two hours** to complete your final written response. You should aim to write 800–1000 words.

You will be allowed to take a copy of the text into the assessment with you providing you have not made any notes in it. You will, however, be allowed to prepare one A4 sheet of your own notes before the assessment and refer to these as you write your final answer.

AO3 Studying written language

- **Read and understand texts, selecting material appropriate to purpose, collating from different sources and making comparisons and cross-references as appropriate.**

  For this part of the assessment, this means that you need to read the whole text and be able to select details from it to support the points you want to make. Making links between different parts of the prose text or play will also help you to put together a stronger answer.

- **Develop and sustain interpretations of writers' ideas and perspectives.**

  As well as being able to write about the text in detail, you also need to get a sound overview of it. This means that you should be comfortable writing about themes in the text and the ideas and opinions expressed by the writer.

- **Explain and evaluate how writers use linguistic, grammatical, structural and presentational features to achieve effects and engage and influence the reader.**
  This means that you will consider how the writer uses language and stylistic features to create particular effects on the reader or audience. You will also write about how the plot is structured and how this structure also works to create meaning.

- **Understand texts in their social, cultural and historical contexts.**
  This point relates to the background of the text. Do you know when and where it is set? How does this influence the way you read and respond to the text?

Check your learning...

Now that you have reached the end of this chapter, take a look at the points below and give yourself a rating of 1 to 4 for each one. '1' means that you still have work to do on this skill, while '4' means that you can perform this skill very well.

Can you...

✔ select details from the text and sometimes cross-reference them with details from different parts of the book?

✔ write about the whole text confidently?

✔ explore characters and themes from the text?

✔ make personal comments based on your own interest in the text?

✔ show a fairly clear awareness of the background context to the text?

Chapter 1.5 — Prose and Drama

Your Assessment

This chapter looks at the skills you need to read and explore longer texts such as novels and plays in order to write about them in an exam. For GCSE English Literature you will have to study **three** long texts to prepare for **two exams**.

The first text will be a **different cultures novel** set by the exam board. This will be assessed in your exam for Unit 1.

The second and third texts will be a **play** and **novel** also set by the exam board. These will be assessed in your exam for Unit 2. One of the texts for Unit 2 will be a 'heritage' text and the other will be a 'contemporary' text.

Learn how to...

- ✔ write about a long text in detail and as a whole in an exam
- ✔ write from the point of view of a character in a text you are studying
- ✔ use close-reading skills to annotate and write about an extract
- ✔ make valid points about characters and themes in the text
- ✔ show that you understand the relevant contexts
- ✔ give a personal response on the text in your answer
- ✔ write from the perspective of a character in a text you are studying.

What are 'Heritage' and 'Contemporary' texts?

Heritage means that the text was written in the past, but is still considered to be important to readers today. **Contemporary** means the text was written in modern times, either the late 20th century or since 2000.

When writing about your texts in the exam, you should try to show how each one fits into the background of when and where it is set. You should always tie these points back to what happens in the text and show how they help you to better understand the characters and events.

Can you write about the detail of your text?

In your exam, you will need to write in detail about the texts you are studying, as well as showing that you know what happens in each text as a whole. To write about the detail of your texts you need to be confident when selecting examples to back up your points.

When writing about a long text, you will need to be **selective**. You can't write about every line or every single thing that happens in the story. Evidence such as quotations should be short and should help you to explain your ideas. You can expand on quotations – perhaps by commenting on the writer's use of language or the themes reflected in the quotation.

Read the extract from the novel *Paddy Clarke Ha Ha Ha* by Roddy Doyle.

Paddy Clarke Ha Ha Ha

I opened the box of Persil and sprinkled some of it on the sea.
Nothing happened really; it just spotted the water and disappeared.
I did it again. I couldn't think of anything else to do with it.
– Give us it, said Kevin.
I did.
He grabbed Edward Swanwick. We grabbed him as well when we saw what he was doing. Edward Swanwick wasn't really a friend of ours.
He was on the edge. I'd never called for him. I'd never been in his kitchen. At Halloween, when we knocked at his house, they never gave us sweets or money – always fruit. And Missis Swanwick warned us to eat it.
– What did she mean?
– It's none of her business what we do with it, said Liam.
We got Edward Swanwick onto the ground and tried to get his mouth open. It was easy; there were ways of doing it. Keeping it open was the problem. Kevin started pouring the Persil onto his face.

Now read the first paragraph from a student's answer below. It was written in response to the following question: 'What do you think about the way Paddy behaves in this extract?'

Student response

Paddy doesn't seem to really think about what he is doing. Kevin decides to pour washing powder over Edward and he just joins in for no reason. Kevin grabs Edward and then Paddy does too: 'We grabbed him as well when we saw what he was doing.' He doesn't really say why he does these things. Paddy seems bored and he often just seems to be trying to think of something new to do. Like at the start of the extract with the washing powder. He says 'I couldn't think of anything else to do with it.' This is why the quick decision from Kevin to bully Edward grabs his attention because it's just something to do. His short answer when Kevin asks him to give him the powder, 'I did', shows that he doesn't really stop to think about what the consequences might be. He only tries to give reasons why he doesn't like Edward after already deciding to go along with it all.

> **How does this student refer to the novel in detail in this answer? Can you suggest ways in which the student could make this response sharper?**

Can you answer a question on a whole text?

To write well about a text as a whole you need to be clear about what **happens** in the story. What happens to all of the main characters by the end? How have they changed? Have they learned anything at all? What are the key events of the plot and in what order do they take place?

When reading and studying your text, keep a note of important themes. Themes are ideas and topics that crop up again and again in texts. Growing up, love, loss and violence are all examples of themes. Writers may have a clear point of view on these topics, or they may present more than one view through the action, the description and what the characters think and say.

For the text you are studying:
- summarize the key events of the text in a list of ten points.
- name three important themes in the text. What does the book say about each theme?

When writing about a text in an exam, you need to deal with the task straight away. Do not start off by explaining what you are going to write about or by writing a long introduction!

Read the openings to two student responses below and on the next page. The first deals with the novel *To Kill a Mockingbird* by Harper Lee and the second focuses on the play *An Inspector Calls*, by J. B. Priestley.

Write about Dill and his importance to the novel as a whole.

Student response

Dill is Scout and Jem's long-term summer holiday friend. 'Dill was from Meridien, Mississippi' and spent 'the summer with his aunt, Miss Rachel.' Dill is short for 'Charles Baker Harris', an embarrassing name to have and the subject of a lot of teasing.

Jem and Scout embrace Dill as their good friend and so demonstrate Atticus's attitude towards people. Atticus's humanity and fair treatment of others is reflected in the way Jem and Scout treat Dill.

The story is also a very serious one, so there is a need for some humour. Dill entertains the readers on a number of occasions within the book. For instance. . .

2 | Who is responsible for Eva Smith's death?

Student response

There are several things that caused Eva Smith's death – the actions and behaviour of Mr and Mrs Birling, and Eva's relationship with Gerald and with Eric. These are the reasons Eva Smith took her own life.

Mr Birling is loud, conceited and a 'hard-headed business man'. He cares mostly about his business and his wealth. . .

Which of the two openings, above and on page 107, do you think is the strongest? Give reasons for your choice.

Can you write about an extract from a text you have studied?

In your exam for Unit 1 and for Unit 2 of your English Literature GCSE, you will have to answer **two** questions on each text you study. One question for each text will be based on an **extract**.

Extract questions test close-reading skills. They are short, sharp tasks which ask you to make key points and give key references. When attempting this type of question, you should focus on the extract by **annotating** it with the question in mind. This simply means reading with a pen in your hand and underlining or circling phrases that are important to the question.

> Choose an extract from one of the texts you are studying. The extract should be about a page in length and should focus on one of the main characters. Pick one of the questions below and annotate the extract with the question in mind:
> - What are your thoughts and feelings as you read the extract?
> - What do you think about how the character speaks and behaves in the extract?

When writing about an extract in the exam, put it quickly in its place in the text. **Do not** drift into writing about the text in general; focus on the extract itself. Your wider knowledge of the text will show.

Make sure you cover the beginning, the middle and the end of the extract. How much time should you spend on this type of question? Answer: **20 minutes!**

> Write an answer to the question you picked above in 20 minutes. Try to use all of the time you have and aim to cover the whole extract.

Writing about prose extracts

The tasks for both drama and prose texts will focus on similar topics. Whatever text you are writing about you need to understand **what the question is asking for**.

Prose and drama texts **both have** characters, relationships and mood and atmosphere. They also both have plot and setting. Extract questions on prose could therefore ask you to focus on any of these topics.

> Select an extract from a prose text that you are studying that you think conveys a strong mood and atmosphere. Explain your choice with reference to the text.

In addition, prose texts have descriptions and a narrator. Importantly, prose also has **readers**. Read the extract below from the novel *Silas Marner* by George Eliot. In the response that follows, a student writes about the impact of the extract on the reader.

Silas Marner

He rose and placed his candle unsuspectingly on the floor near his loom, swept away the sand without noticing any change, and removed the bricks. The sight of the empty hole made his heart leap violently, but the belief that his gold was gone could not come at once – only terror, and the eager effort to put an end to the terror. He passed his trembling hand all about the hole, trying to think it possible that his eyes had deceived him; then he held the candle in the hole and examined it curiously, trembling more and more. At last he shook so violently that he let fall the candle, and lifted his hands to his head, trying to steady himself, that he might think.

Student response

. . .The reader sees the grief that Silas has when the truth sets in when his physical reaction becomes shocking to the reader: 'trembling more and more'. When Silas shakes so much that he drops the candle it shows any previous joy and luxury in his miserable life has gone out. All light is put out (the gold in his life taken). It is hard not to feel quite sad for him. . .

Discuss how the section of the student's answer above would impress an examiner. How would you continue the response?

Read the extract below. What impact is this extract likely to have on the reader? Write a response with close reference to the text.

A Christmas Carol

The yard was so dark that even Scrooge, who knew its every stone, was fain to grope with his hands. The fog and frost so hung about the black old gateway of the house, that it seemed as if the Genius of the Weather sat in mournful meditation on the threshold.

Now, it is a fact that there was nothing at all particular about the knocker on the door, except that it was very large. It is also a fact that Scrooge had seen it, night and morning, during his whole residence in that place; also that Scrooge had as little of what is called fancy about him as any man in the city of London, even including – which is a bold word – the corporation, aldermen, and livery. Let it also be borne in mind that Scrooge had not bestowed one thought on Marley since his last mention of his seven-years' dead partner that afternoon. And then let any man explain to me, if he can, how it happened that Scrooge, having his key in the lock of the door, saw in the knocker, without its undergoing any intermediate process of change – not a knocker, but Marley's face.

Marley's face. It was not in impenetrable shadow, as the other objects in the yard were, but had a dismal light about it, like a bad lobster in a dark cellar. It was not angry or ferocious, but looked at Scrooge as Marley used to look; with ghostly spectacles turned up on its ghostly forehead. The hair was curiously stirred, as if by breath or hot air; and, though the eyes were wide open, they were perfectly motionless. That, and its livid colour, made it horrible; but its horror seemed to be part of the face and beyond its control, rather than part of its own expression.

As Scrooge looked fixedly at this phenomenon, it was a knocker again.

EXAMINER'S TIP

■ In the exam, you must show that you know and understand your set books. When writing your answer, you should look closely at details of language and the way a text is organized and constructed.

Writing about drama extracts

In addition to some of the features mentioned earlier, drama has actors, directors, stages and audiences. It also has **stage directions** and sound effects and **acts and scenes**. A drama text could also have a narrator.

In drama, you have the added factor of the **audience**. Remember, the plays you study are written to be performed in front of an audience. This means that you are likely to be asked a question about the audience rather than the reader.

> **Select an extract from a drama text that you are studying that you think would have a strong impact on an audience. Explain your choice with reference to the text.**

Controlling your quotations

When answering an extract-based question, remember that you will have the extract in front of you and you should be prepared to support your points with references to it. You should select quotations wisely. Only include a quotation where it is relevant to the point you want to make. Make sure it adds something to your answer. Don't use a quotation to simply repeat something you have already said in your own words. For example:

Sheila accepts that Eva died a horrible death' she says 'she's just died a horrible death'.

Make your quotations work for you – what do they reveal? A better way of making the point above might be:

Sheila accepts that Eva died a 'horrible death'.

This perhaps shows she has at least some sympathy for Eva.

Short quotations are often more effective than longer quotes. Do not get into the habit of copying out large chunks of text just to make your answer seem longer!

How does the student use quotations effectively below?

Student response

...Lennie looks up to George, and he 'imitated him exactly'. George seems to be the only person in Lennie's life so he wants to be the same as him. He likes to be accepted and praised by George, so he adjusts his hat precisely so that it was 'the way George's hat was'...

The writer's skills

Whatever question you are answering, you should always be thinking about **how** the writer uses his or her skills to create effects. What language has the writer chosen to use? Is the writer skilful when it comes to creating a particular atmosphere? Do you sympathize with the characters. Why?

Read the student response below about *To Kill a Mockingbird*.

Student response

As soon as the extract begins, the writer creates a tense atmosphere by using words which emphasize Scout's struggle, and thus showing how her resistance is already futile: 'pulled', 'tried'. This sense of futility and growing tension is increased when Scout tries to reason with Jem and put him off going back. Jem's speech is slow and firm, showing he won't change his mind:

"'That's what I know," said Jem. "That's why I'm goin' after 'em."'

This statement of intent alone sounds menacing, and the growing sense of danger is fuelled when the writer simply adds, 'I began to feel sick'. The simplicity of the language allows the reader to use his/her imagination (and knowledge of previous goings on) to anticipate what is likely to happen, and also to fearfully consider the results of this.

What skills does this student comment on in the response?

Giving a personal response

When responding to an extract question, be prepared to give your own opinions. Some questions may ask you to do this directly by prompting you to explain your **impressions**. Alternatively, you may be asked to explain what your **thoughts and feelings** are in response to a certain event, a character or a relationship between characters.

Following the question, there is likely to be some extra advice, such as:

- Give reasons for what you say, and remember to support your answer with words and phrases from the text.
- Write about words and phrases you find effective in creating these thoughts and feelings and explain why you find them effective.

Make sure you follow this advice in your answer.

Can you write from the point of view of a character?

In your exam, you may be asked to show your understanding of the text you are studying by imagining a character's deep and serious thoughts. Read the sample exam question and student response below.

Imagine you are George. Write down his thoughts sometime after Lennie's death.

Student response

I often got fed up of Lennie but I loved him. I always got frustrated at him when he was so forgetful, I hadda repeat myself several times, and Lennie always being so apologetic all the time. Though Lennie, he listened to me and he did remember 'the dream'. That was one thing he would never forget. The rabbits and to live off the 'fatta the lan'...

> **In the piece of writing on the previous page, what clues are there that the 'voice' sounds a bit like George?**

When writing your own response to the same kind of exam question, you should focus on describing what your character thinks about other characters and what he or she thinks about what has happened in the story.

When writing from the point of view of a character, you need to:
- speak directly as the character
- think like the character
- get into the character's feelings.

The questions will often ask you to write as if you are looking back from the end of the story. This means that everything that happens in the text will have already taken place.

In your answer, you should refer to events or to conversations that the character took part in. Try not to refer to anything that the character would **not** be aware of.

> **Pick a key character from a text you are studying and answer the question below.**

Imagine you are the character. At the end of the story, you think back over what has happened. Write about your thoughts and feelings.

EXAMINER'S TIP

- In simple terms, to write from the point of view of a character means to write in the first person. This means you would expect to use 'I', 'me' and 'my' as you write from the standpoint of your character.

Creating a convincing character

To write an effective response to the type of question above, you need to make sure that the character's thoughts and feelings are believable and in line with what you already know about the character from reading the text.

In the opening to a response below, a student writes from the perspective of the character Alfieri from the play *A View from the Bridge* by Arthur Miller. The question is also included below.

> Imagine you are Alfieri. Write down your thoughts and feelings at the end of the play.

Student response

When Eddie first arrived at my office, I immediately sensed that he was unhappy. I had always suspected that his feelings for Catherine ran much deeper than ordinary guardian love, but it was not my place to express these suspicions. However, after that doomed day, Eddie abandoned all other hopes and committed the ultimate betrayal. However much I convince myself that I was powerless to prevent him, I often wonder if I should have acted more...

How does the response above create a convincing sense of character?

Showing knowledge of the text

When writing about a character's thoughts and feelings, remember that what you write should be based on what actually happens in the text. Do not set out to rewrite the ending! This type of task is an excellent way to show the examiner that you know and understand your text really well.

> **Read the sample task and student response below. How does this student build details from the text into the writing?**

> Imagine you are Atticus. Write down your thoughts after the trial of Tom Robinson.

Student response

It was the last few days of the trial and I felt great anticipation, but at the same time I felt like I was fighting an already lost battle. When the trial started, the first person I questioned was Mr Tate the local sheriff. He seemed quite nervous when I spoke to him as if he was hiding something, but I do not know what. I asked him what eye did Mayella have bruising on, he was not sure, and then he realized that it must have been the left. I realized at that moment that it would have been difficult for Tom to hit her when one of his arms was crippled.

> ### EXAMINER'S TIP
>
> ■ Revise intelligently. Even if you do not write many practice answers, do make sure that you think through possible questions and how you would deal with them. Work out a sound position on as many questions as possible, so that you can start a response with some purpose.

Can you write an essay on a text you have studied?

The essay questions in your exam will require you to answer a question on a whole book. You will have a choice of two essay questions in the exam and you must answer **one** of them. You will also have to answer **one** question on an extract from the text.

Before you go into your exam, you need to make sure you know:

- how the book begins and develops, and particularly how it ends and why
- who the key characters are, what makes them tick and how they behave to each other
- a bit about the time and place in which the text is set and the background to the story.

> **Make a page of notes for each of the texts you are studying with answers to the points listed above. You could use the following sub-headings to arrange your notes:**
> - **Beginning and ending**
> - **Key characters**
> - **Background.**

You also need to have an overall sense of what the writer is trying to say and what messages he or she is giving about life.

> **What are the main messages of the texts you are studying? Discuss your views in small groups.**

In the exam, it is important that you spend **40 minutes** on the essay question for your text because it is worth **20 marks**. You should allow time to think before you start to write.

Writing a purposeful opening

Ensure that your answer deals directly with the question. Make your first point early. Don't spend time explaining what you are going to write about.

The response below includes the opening lines of an answer on *Silas Marner* by George Eliot. This answer was written in response to the following essay question:

> Which character do you think makes the best father in the novel?

Student response

A father should have a close relationship with his children and he should be a role model to them. There are three main fathers in the novel, Silas Marner, Godfrey and Squire Cass. I believe that Silas Marner is the best father-figure in the novel. He gives Eppie plenty of love, she is protected by him and he lets her learn from her own mistakes...

How would the opening of this answer impress an examiner?

EXAMINER'S TIP

- Be cool under pressure and start your response thoughtfully. Make your opening sentences and opening paragraph meaningful to win the confidence of the examiner.
- When writing the main part of your answer, do so in clear sentences. Once you have made a point, move on to the next.

Using the bullet-point support

In the exam, the essay question may include a list of bullet points. These points will suggest what you should cover in your answer. Look at the example exam question below.

An Inspector Calls is set in 1912, and was written in the mid 1940s. Why do you think it is still popular today, in the 21st century?

Think about:

- what happens;
- the way the characters speak and behave at different points in the play;
- the messages of the play;
- what makes the play exciting and dramatic for an audience.

You should follow the points closely. Try to give equal coverage to each point in your answer and use them to structure your writing. Look at the opening lines of four paragraphs from one student's response below.

Student response

'An Inspector Calls' is about a young woman called Eva Smith who is neglected by an entire family. No one will take responsibility for her. . .

Every member of the family is quizzed by the Inspector. Each one is shown to be in denial, but has to face the truth eventually. Mr and Mrs Birling...

There are some strong messages from the play, and they are still relevant in the 21st century. Mr Birling shouldn't be able to buy privileges over others. His family. . .

It is exciting and dramatic for the audience because all of the family are at odds. . .

How has this student used the bullet points to organize their answer?

Using the key words of the question

Some of the questions set in the exam may not have bullet points. Instead, you need to build a very simple essay structure from the key words in the question.

Before you begin your answer, read the question closely and underline the key words in it. Look at the example below.

> Write about two or three parts of the play that you think an audience would find particularly amusing, and explain why they would have that effect.

For this question, you need to write about at least two or three different parts of the text. You need to select parts that you think the audience would find amusing and you need to explore **why** this is the case.

You should refer back to the key words as you write your answer to focus your writing.

- **Make a list of the key words in each essay question below.**
- **Choose one of the questions and write a response based on a text you are studying.**

- Write about the relationship between two of the characters in the text and explain how it changes at different points.

- What are your thoughts and feelings about one of the characters and the way he or she speaks and behaves at different points in the text?

- Explain the importance of one of the characters in the text as a whole.

EXAMINER'S TIP

- Always answer the question set. Do not answer the question you were hoping to get OR the one that you answered in the 'mock' exam!

Including evidence from the text

As this is a closed-book exam, you will not have a copy of the text to refer to when writing your response to the essay question. You will be given an extract to answer the extract-based question, but you should not rely on this when writing your essay response. Your essay response needs to range across the text as a whole.

In your essay, you will need to back up your points with evidence. This does not mean that you have to memorize hundreds of quotations! Short, one-or-two-word quotations can be very effective. Look out for key phrases that might be useful as you read and study your text before the exam.

You can also use **paraphrasing** to support your points. You should not set out to re-tell the story. Good use of paraphrasing is simply a case of picking out one or two examples from the text to illustrate your point. Read the response below on *A Christmas Carol* by Charles Dickens.

Student response

Scrooge's immediate disregard for other human beings shows his attitude towards the poor; how he sees them as a waste of space and if they don't have money, they can't be happy. Scrooge continues to call the poor 'not his business'.

As the last spirit appears, the ghost of Christmas yet to come, Scrooge is prepared for change, 'hear me! I am not the man I was!' Scrooge's language is clear, he is admitting to being a selfish old man and is now ready to change. With each spirit Scrooge's opinion on Christmas and the poor change.

How has the student used quotations effectively in the response above? Where has the student used paraphrasing effectively?

Finishing your essay

Keep track of the time available throughout your exam and aim to finish on time. Finish your essay by summing up your overall view in response to the question. Try to draw together everything that you have written but do not repeat yourself.

Look at the sample question below and the last paragraph of a response.

> Is jealousy to blame for the tragic events in *Othello*?

Student response

I believe that the tragic events in 'Othello' were not solely because of jealousy. I believe that there were other reasons that led to the tragedy's ending. I think that jealousy was part of it but that it was a combination of other emotions too, such as love and misunderstanding, mixed with fate and luck, which caused the horrendous events to take place.

How does the student tie the answer back to the question? What else makes this an effective finishing paragraph?

EXAMINER'S TIP

- When answering an essay question, think in terms of overview and detail. Show that you are in touch with the writer's ideas and that you know different parts of the text well enough to impress.

Exam Practice I

Extract question

Paddy Clarke Ha Ha Ha

In your exam, you will have to answer an extract-based question on each text you have studied. In your exam for Unit 1, you will answer an extract-based question on a different cultures prose text. In your Unit 2 exam, you will answer a separate extract-based question on both the prose and the drama text you have studied for the unit.

The sample task below is based on an extract from the prose text *Paddy Clarke Ha Ha Ha* by Roddy Doyle.

The tide was going out so we'd be getting out in a minute. Edward Swanwick pushed his hands out and sent a wave towards me and there was a jellyfish in it. A huge see-through one with pink veins and a purple middle. I lifted my arms way up and started to move but it still rubbed my side. I screamed. I pushed through the water to the steps. I felt the jellyfish hit my back; I thought I did. I yelled again; I couldn't help it. It was rocky and uneven down at the seafront, not like the beach. I got to the steps and grabbed the bar.

– It's a Portuguese man of war, said Edward Swanwick.

He was coming back to the steps a long way, around the jellyfish.

I got onto the second step. I looked for marks. Jellyfish stings didn't hurt until you got out of the water. There was a pink lash on the side of my belly; I could see it. I was out of the water.

– I'm going to get you, I told Edward Swanwick.

– It's a Portuguese man of war, said Edward Swanwick.

– Look at it.

I showed him my wound.

He was up on the platform now, looking over the railing at the jellyfish.

I took my togs off without bothering with a towel. There was no one else. The jellyfish was still floating there, like a runny umbrella. Edward Swanwick was hunting for stones. He went down some of the steps to reach for some but he wouldn't get back into the water. I couldn't get my T-shirt down over my back and chest because I was wet. It was stuck on my shoulders.

– Their stings are poisonous, said Edward Swanwick.

I had my T-shirt on now. I lifted it to make sure the mark was still there. I thought it was beginning to get sore.

---

1. **Paddy Clarke Ha Ha Ha**

   *Answer part (a) and **either** part (b) **or** part (c).*
   You are advised to spend about 20 minutes on part (a), and about
   40 minutes on part (b) or part (c).

   (a) Read the extract on the opposite page. Then answer the following question:

   What are your impressions of Paddy in this extract? [10]

Sample answer

Read the sample student answer below and comments from the examiner on the next page.

Student response to Question (a)

Paddy doesn't seem very nice in this passage. He is a bit of a baby and likes attention from everyone. When he is playing in the water with Edward, he overreacts when the jellyfish comes towards him. 'I screamed... I yelled again; I couldn't help it.' He gets really angry with Edward even though it wasn't really Edward's fault, it was an accident. He behaves really childishly towards Edward and Paddy is not very nice towards him: 'I'm going to get you, I told Edward Swanwick.'

Paddy also comes across as being a big baby when he goes home to see his mother after this part in the novel. He seems to be making a fuss over nothing. I'm not even sure if he was stung by the jellyfish because no one else seems to be able to see the mark except him. At the end of this extract for example, he says: 'I thought it was beginning to get sore'. He says 'I thought', which suggests he's not even sure if it's really hurting him.

Paddy definitely comes across as an attention seeker. He's keen to let everyone know that he has been injured by the jellyfish. Edward seems to be very interested by the jellyfish, saying what type it is and trying to get a better look. Paddy interrupts, however, to try and get him to notice his 'wound'. Before he went home he checked to 'make sure the mark was still there'. It is clear that he wants to use it to try and be the centre of attention.

Exam Practice 2

Empathy question

Of Mice and Men

In your exam for Unit 1 and Unit 2, you **may** be given a task that asks you to write from the perspective of one of the characters in a text you have studied. This is sometimes referred to as an 'empathy' question. In addition to one extract-based question, which you **must** answer, you will also have a **choice** of two further questions and you must answer **one** of them.

The sample exam question that follows is based on the novel *Of Mice and Men* by John Steinbeck.

Either,

(b) Imagine you are Slim. What are your thoughts as you look back on the events at the ranch involving George and Lennie?   [20]

Or,

(c) Imagine you are George. Write down your thoughts and feelings about:

- the events that were most important to you;
- your relationship with Lennie;
- your relationship with other characters;
- what lessons you have learnt.   [20]

Sample answer

Read the sample student answer below and comments from the examiner on the next page.

I remember the whole business now. Of course, George still works here on the ranch. After Lennie died, he eventually decided to try to hold down a job. But the spark's gone from him now – he and Lennie were more than just travelling companions. They were closer than I've ever seen two guys.

The incident affected many people on the ranch pretty badly – probably George worst of all. After he shot Lennie, I took him for a drink and tried to console him. But George just threw down whiskey after whiskey and didn't say much; from time to time he mumbled the odd sentence about a childhood memory. But hell, I don't think I've ever seen a guy so down and depressed. I know it was the right thing to do – Curley would have had Lennie strung up or shot him in the guts. But that wouldn't have been no good. Candy was hit very badly – he got the can two weeks later and was very upset, not only because he'd lost a friend in Lennie, but because of something else which he told me about in private soon after. It seems that George, Lennie and Candy were one month away from packing in their jobs and buying their own place. Every ranch worker has their own dream, but that's the closest I've ever seen anyone come to achieving it.

The boss wasn't particularly happy at losing Lennie either – he said he thought that Lennie was the best damn worker we've ever had on this ranch. He was certainly the strongest. The boss apparently didn't trust the pair of them when they first turned up, but one day when he saw Lennie shifting barley bags into a cart, and lifting them as if they were feathers, damn nearly killing the two men struggling behind him, he was won over. I was certainly pleased to have such a good worker on my team – it made life a whole lot easier and made a change from the pair of punks that he had replaced.

I was shocked when I saw the reaction of Carlson and the others after Lennie had died – they couldn't understand why George was so depressed. The man had just shot his best friend – surely that's reason enough to be slightly unhappy. I think I understood what George was going through, but there was really very little I could do other than listen to him.

Of course, Curley's wife was buried the next day. I always felt sorry for her – she was always so lost, lonely and out of place, being the only woman on the ranch. I never thought Curley looked after her – and because of that and her flirting all the time, I guess she was a death trap waiting to happen. Curley, that heartless good-for-nothing, didn't even shed a tear at the funeral. Even when he had just seen his own wife killed, and I advised him to stay with her, he seemed more concerned with settling an old score with Lennie. Sure enough, he's already been seen strutting around the ranch with a new woman – I only hope she doesn't go the same way.

Lennie was only with us for a short time, but even that seemed to pass very quickly. I could see from the beginning that, although he was dumb as hell, he was a nice guy deep down, and would never deliberately hurt anyone.

EXAMINER'S COMMENT

This is a superb answer. It sounds like Slim from beginning to end. His thoughts and feelings show clear insight into many of the other characters in the novel and their relationships. The student's knowledge of the text shines through consistently, with excellent selection of detail. Slim is sensitive, but no fool. The invented details are okay because they too contribute to what Slim says about other characters. This is a full-marks answer – with a lot to spare!

Exam Practice 3

Essay question

Paddy Clarke Ha Ha Ha

As well as an extract-based question on each text, you will have to answer a question on each text as a whole. This **may** take the form of an essay question. You will have a **choice** of two essay questions per text and you must answer **one** of them.

The sample exam question below is based on the novel *Paddy Clarke Ha Ha Ha* by Roddy Doyle.

Either,

(b) Write about the relationship between Paddy and his father and explain how it changes. Think about:
   *   their relationship at the start of the novel;
   *   the way their relationship develops and changes;
   *   the reasons for the way their relationship develops and changes;
   *   the way they speak and behave at different points in the novel. [20]

Or,

(c) '*Paddy Clarke Ha Ha Ha* is a story about learning from experience.'
   Write about some incidents from the novel that you think either
   support or do not support this statement. Give reasons for what you say. [20]

Sample answer

Read the sample student answer below and comments from the examiner on the next page.

Student response to Question (b)

I think Paddy knows something is not right when he hears the television, which means that his parents are 'still downstairs' and not in bed. Paddy has heard his parents arguing before and it disturbs him. I think at this point he is scared of his father. His father was the only one he could hear.

Paddy knows when they argue, because of the tone of their voice and how they talk to each other, 'like screamed whispers'. Paddy is upset by his parents fighting. He gets cold as he sits on the stairs and listens to them, but he has to stay and listen. He is desperate to make them stop.

The first exchange between Paddy and his father is when Paddy has a magnifying glass. His father is trying his best to be fatherly but Paddy doesn't know how to react to him.

There is awkwardness between Paddy and his father. When Paddy asks about Granda Clarke's house, we see the more gentle side of Paddy's Da.

When Paddy is questioning his father about the book 'The Naked and the Dead', his father suddenly seems rather standoffish. This could just be because he is reading and doesn't want to talk, but I think it is because he is quite moody and changeable; this is why Paddy doesn't know how to react with him.

In certain parts of the book, we see how Paddy is studying his father. He describes his father's hands in great detail and compares them to his. Paddy is very perceptive and he knows the mood of his father well: 'He sometimes liked these questions, and sometimes he didn't'.

The point where the relationship between Paddy and his father breaks down is the moment Paddy sees his Da hitting his Ma. At that moment he loses all respect for him and begins to dislike him. Finally, at the end of the novel, we see the distance between Paddy and his father. They no longer have anything to say to each other. Paddy has grown up a lot since his father left and he no longer has incessant questions for his father. They just shake hands and it is very cold and impersonal. Paddy no longer has any connection with his father: 'His hands felt cold and big, dry and hard.'

EXAMINER'S COMMENT

This is a very strong answer that covers all four bullet points given in the question. This student uses an effective mixture of paraphrase and short quotations to support the points made. This student shows an extremely good knowledge of what happens in the novel and is able to range confidently across it, picking parts that best illustrate the developing relationship between Paddy and his father. On a technical level, this response is also very well written. The sentences are clear and sharp and the paragraphs are well organized; an excellent response.

How is prose and drama assessed at GCSE?

Use the questions below to check your performance when studying and writing about literary prose and drama texts.

Does the response...
- ❑ show some personal response to the text and general knowledge of the story?
- ❑ show some selection of relevant detail to support points?
- ❑ discuss characters and relationships thoughtfully?
- ❑ discuss wider themes in the text and provide examples?
- ❑ deal confidently with the whole text, with an overview and ability to move from the specific to the general?

Are there...
- ❑ simple comments about language choices?
- ❑ simple comments on particular features of style and structure?
- ❑ comments about how different aspects of style and structure help to create effects, meanings and ideas?
- ❑ developed comments on language, structure and form exploring meaning and effects?

Is there...
- ❑ a selection of simple comments on the background of the text?
- ❑ a clear grasp of the relevant social, cultural and historical contexts?
- ❑ some consideration of the importance of social, cultural and historical contexts when reading and responding to the text?
- ❑ a clear selection of evidence from the text, which is used to support a clear understanding of the relevant social, cultural and historical contexts?

Is the expression (the grammar, punctuation and spelling)...
- ❑ likely to make the response unclear in places?
- ❑ reasonably clear with a good basic sense of structure?
- ❑ mainly clear with only minor errors?
- ❑ clear and fluent, with few errors in grammar, punctuation and spelling?

Preparing for the exam

Here is a summary of the important information from the GCSE Literature specification for studying and writing about literary prose and drama texts. This section includes the relevant Assessment Objectives, which show you how your work will be marked.

GCSE ENGLISH LITERATURE UNIT 1: Prose (different cultures) and poetry (contemporary)

Section A: Different cultures prose (21%)

Examination

Your examination for Unit 1 is divided into two sections. **Section A** will assess you on a different cultures prose text and **Section B** will assess you on unseen poetry. For Section A, you will have to answer **two** questions on the text you have studied. The first question (part (a)) will be based on an extract from the text.

The second question will offer a **choice** of two tasks (part (b) and part (c)). Both questions will relate to the text as a whole and you must answer **one** of them.

In this book, Section B is covered in Chapter 1.2.

AO1

- **Respond to texts critically and imaginatively; select and evaluate relevant textual detail to illustrate and support interpretations.**
  This means that you need to read the whole text and be able to select details from it to support the points you want to make. You need to be confident when giving your own opinions and comfortable explaining the views and ideas expressed by the writer.

AO2

- **Explain how language, structure and form contribute to writers' presentation of ideas, themes and settings.**
  This means that you will consider how the writer uses language and stylistic features to create particular effects on the reader. You will also write about how events are structured in the novel and how this structure works to create meaning.

AO4

- **Relate texts to their social, cultural and historical contexts; explain how texts have been influential and significant to self and other readers in different contexts and at different times.**
  This point relates to the background of the novel. How does it fit in with the writer's background and the time and place in which the text was written? Do you know when and where the text is set? How does this influence the way you read and respond to the characters and events?

GCSE ENGLISH LITERATURE UNIT 2a: Literary heritage drama and contemporary prose

GCSE ENGLISH LITERATURE UNIT 2b: Contemporary drama and literary heritage prose

Individual texts in context (40%)

Examination

You will answer **two** questions on each of the texts that you have studied for this unit. One text will be a prose text and the other will be a drama text. For each text, the first question (part (i)) will require you to base your answer on an extract that will be printed on the exam paper.

The second question will offer a **choice** of two tasks (part (ii) and part (iii)). For both the drama and the prose, both of these tasks will relate to the text as a whole and you must choose to answer one of them.

You will have **two hours** to complete a total of four responses on two separate texts.

AO1

- **Respond to texts critically and imaginatively; select and evaluate relevant textual detail to illustrate and support interpretations.**
  This means that you need to read each text and be able to select details from it to support the points you want to make. You need to be confident when giving your own opinions about each text and comfortable explaining the views and ideas expressed by the writer.

AO2

- **Explain how language, structure and form contribute to writers' presentation of ideas, themes and settings.**
  This means that you will consider how writers use language and stylistic features to create particular effects on the reader. You will also write about how events are structured in the texts you study and how the structure works to create meaning.

AO4

- **Relate texts to their social, cultural and historical contexts; explain how texts have been influential and significant to self and other readers in different contexts and at different times.**
  This point relates to the background of the texts you study for this unit. How does each text fit in with the writer's background and the time and place in which each text was written? Do you know when and where each text is set? How does this influence the way you read and respond to the characters and events?

Reading a text independently

You will be a much stronger English Literature exam candidate if you are able and willing to read your set texts outside of lessons. You should keep a record of your response to each text as these thoughts and impressions are guaranteed to be of use to you later. The following questions may help you to keep track of your ideas.

The plot

- What happens at the start of the text? What do you think of the opening?
- How do you expect the plot to develop? What are the key stages of the plot?
- How do you expect the story to end? What do you think of the ending?
- Are any questions left unanswered?

The characters

- How important is each character in the plot?
- How do some of the characters change as the story develops?
- Are there any moments when you feel strongly for or against particular characters?
- Do the various locations/settings of the story cause the characters to behave differently?

Themes

- What do you think the main themes are in the text and how do they develop?
- How do the actions of the main characters link to these ideas?
- What do you think the writer is trying to say about the themes?

The writer

- What issues do you think the writer is interested in dealing with in the text?
- Do you notice any particular features that stand out in the writer's style of writing?
- Is there anything interesting about the way the writer has chosen to arrange and organize the story?

Writing effectively with accuracy

Even though Unit 1 and Unit 2 both deal with your reading skills, the quality of your writing skills will still play a significant part in your performance in your exams. Good control of your written expression will get the examiner on your side and will influence their overall judgment of your work.

You will perform better if you:
- put your ideas across clearly
- organize your writing using sentences and paragraphs
- use a wide range of vocabulary
- use the grammar of Standard English
- use accurate spelling
- use accurate punctuation
- present your work neatly.

Most important of all, your writing should have a sense of purpose – in other words, answer the question as set. Do not repeat the essay you wrote in the mock exam and do not offload, thoughtlessly, everything you know about your set books. Ensure that everything you write relates to the question.

Check your learning...

Having now reached the end of this chapter, assess your progress by awarding yourself a rating from 1 to 4 for each of the points below. '1' means that you still have work to do on this skill, while '4' means that you can perform this skill very well.

Can you...

- ✔ make detailed reference to your books?
- ✔ use close-reading skills to answer questions based on extracts?
- ✔ discuss characters and relationships thoughtfully?
- ✔ write from the perspective of a character from a text?
- ✔ explore the deeper meanings of the texts with some confidence?
- ✔ discuss ideas, themes, places and times?
- ✔ put your ideas across clearly?

Chapter 2.1

Creative Writing

Your Assessment

LA **E**

This chapter looks at the skills required to write creatively and with accuracy. You will be assessed on these skills by Controlled Assessment, where you will need to complete **two tasks** under formal supervision.

If you are studying **GCSE English Language**, you will have to complete one piece of **descriptive writing** and one piece of **narrative writing**. Descriptive means that you must focus on a scene or a person; narrative requires you to tell a short story.

If you are studying **GCSE English**, you will produce one piece of **first-person writing** and one piece of **third-person writing**. First-person writing mainly uses 'I'; third-person writing mainly uses 'he' or 'she'.

Learn how to...

✔ use your imagination to write creatively
✔ write in controlled sentences with attention to punctuation
✔ choose your words carefully to express your meaning
✔ write a focused piece of descriptive writing
✔ write a sensible piece of narrative writing
✔ write from a first-person and third-person perspective.

Using your imagination

If you're doing a GCSE seriously, you need to be serious about your writing. That does not mean serious to the point of being dull, but it does mean you have to avoid childish imaginative stories about monsters, outer space and saving the world from evil.

Daring your best friend to go into the haunted house at the end of your street at night? Well, that piece of writing has been done time and time again and done badly!

However, you do not have to write about yourself to be successful. You can write realistically about fictional places and fictional events. In other words, you can make things up that can still be believable.

The best approach to the tasks in this chapter is to write about places and events that are reasonably close to your own experience and knowledge of the world. Attempt the activity below to challenge your imagination.

- In groups of three, cut out headlines and phrases from newspapers and magazines and scatter them on the table. Each person picks three cuttings.
- Write a story of at least three paragraphs, making use of the cuttings you have selected. Use either the exact words or the subject matter.
- Your piece of writing must have a title, an opening, a closing paragraph and accurate punctuation and grammar.

Descriptive writing

For **GCSE English Language**, you will need to produce **one** piece of **descriptive writing**. The task will usually require you to describe a place or an event that is likely to be familiar to you.

When writing a piece of descriptive writing the key word to remember is **focus**; this means making sure you meet the requirements of the task. Don't set out to write a story.

Can you write a focused piece of description?

Your description needs to be engaging and believable. You need to create a proper sense of place. Begin by forming a picture in your head and then try to put this into words. Often it is the little details, such as people and movement in the scene, which can help to bring your writing to life.

It is also important not to overdo the description – senses, adjectives, similes and metaphors are useful, but not as important as sentence control and clear punctuation.

Read the opening from a student response below. These opening lines were written in response to the title 'In town'.

Student response

It was midday. The sun was high in the sky and burning bright. Happy shoppers were pacing up and down the high street.

Can you add three more sentences to the opening above, adding further detail to the description of the scene?

Can you write an effective opening?

Openings are very important because the reader's interest can be won or lost, and so can marks in exams! The writer needs to start well, writing accurately and convincingly.

Ask yourself the following questions as you write:
- Is the description believable and realistic?
- Is the writing controlled and precise?

The openings that appear on the next page were written in response to the following descriptive writing task:

> You are on a bus which has stopped because of road works. Describe the scene.

Read the openings and discuss the strengths and weaknesses of each one. Which one do you think is the most effective and why?

Student response 1

It was 9.30 sharp. The big, bright, bulky yellow bus came to an immediate stop. There were noises like never before: big burly men in yellow tops were making a racket like an earthquake erupting. The smell of tar and traffic fumes intermingled creating a disgusting aroma and the bombardment of visual pollution took over the fabulous green countryside.

ROAD AHEAD CLOSED

Student response 2

There was the sound of panicking. There was a sudden stop. People making phone calls and a big hole in the ground. Men working outside and it was impossible to think. The sound went through us and the taste of dust scattered around through the open windows. The smell of burning and the heat flared on us. The smell of tar and the smell of sweat remained on the bus.

Student response 3

The bus hadn't moved for fifteen minutes. Laughter and chatter could be heard from the bottom of the bus while the wails and cries could be heard from the tiny babies hungry for food. The hopeless conductor tired of calming and assuring sat down on to one of the rugged, broken and vandalised chairs. The bus groaned to a sudden stop. Outside, the horns of impatient drivers could be heard. There were shouts of emphasized sarcasm filled with impatience, anger and worry.

> **Choose one of the following tasks and write an opening of three or four sentences.**
> - **Describe the scene at a busy hairdresser's salon.**
> - **Write a description of a park in winter.**
> - **Describe a queue for a popular ride at a theme park.**

Can you write in controlled sentences with attention to punctuation?

Your writing is guaranteed to make a better impression on the examiner if it is constructed out of clear controlled sentences with accurate punctuation. You can also make your writing more interesting by varying your sentences.

Make use of the following tips:
- **Stop** at the end of sentences – with full stops, question marks or exclamation marks.
- **Slow** the pace of sentences – with commas, semi-colons, brackets and dashes.

> **Improve the response below by punctuating it with full stops and capital letters.**

Student response

I was going to Blackpool beach with my family for a day out we had arrived at 11.00 am it was summer and it was boiling the water was warm and the sand was soft I got out of the car after what seemed two hours of torture gasping for breath I looked around the sand felt soft against my feet and the sea was shining crystal clear blue the sun was shining down and the heat was unbearable

Now take a look at a second piece of writing. This was written in response to a task entitled 'A local walk'.

Student response

As we wandered down alongside the river with our dog to keep us company. We was taking in the beautiful views of the countryside. As we let off the lead he ran away down the river into the trees.

The lines above are not hopeless, but they are perhaps a bit thoughtless. In terms of grammar, the first sentence is unfinished (caused by 'as') and the second sentence has a basic error ('We was'). In terms of descriptive detail, there is very little sense of a particular place, event or occasion.

> - **How could you make this piece of writing more accurate and effective?**
> - **Write an improved version of this paragraph.**

Can you choose your words carefully?

Choosing the right words can make all the difference in a piece of descriptive writing. Words have the power to convert a bland page of text into a vivid scene in the mind of the reader!

> **What can you do to improve each of the sentences below?**

1. When an aeroplane went by one of the kids went absolutely ballistic.

2. The runway was big and looked hot from the sun.

3. A woman at the check-in desk said, "Can I see your ticket?"

EXAMINER'S TIP

■ When putting together a piece of descriptive writing, avoid using slang. For example: 'We was late'; 'I got beat'; 'Pass them socks', etc. Forget your text messaging and forget habits of speech. Try to select words that enable you to put your ideas across precisely.

Can you spell most words correctly?

Good spelling is a case of checking your work and making an effort to learn how to spell words that you often get wrong. You need to make sure that you have simple words sorted. This includes words such as *where/wear/were, here/hear* and *there/their*. Make sure you know what all of these words mean and when it is correct to use each one.

Learn the patterns in regular words. Know when to use double consonants and where silent letters appear. Make sure you use the correct vowels in words and also the correct order of vowels. For example: *beautiful, business* and *receive*.

> **Make a list of ten words that you find difficult to spell. Look these words up, and write down the correct spelling of each one. Do you notice any patterns in the words you have listed? Are there any rules you could learn to help you spell these words correctly?**

When writing and checking your work, avoid silly errors with apostrophes. For example, apostrophes should **not** be used to show that a noun is plural. For example: egg becomes eggs **not** egg's.

Can you write out the sentences below correctly?

I didnt no what I was doin. Their must of been hundreds of people. My whole school was their aswell.

Can you check and correct your writing?

Taking what you have learned into account, how could you improve each piece of writing below? Pay attention to the punctuation, grammar and spelling.

Make a list of corrections and suggestions for each response.

Student response 1

The cinema

Everyone was smiling and enjoying themselves well the kids were anyway when the cinema doors open all the kids rushed in. There was a big counter seling popcorn and sweets outside and lots of kids were queing up to get there treats. As the lights went out the film was about to start.

Student response 2

A rainy day in town

The sky was packed with grey clouds. People were hurridly trying to get into a shop or undercover. Benches and paths where left desserted as many people cramed into small shops. Then the rain was falling heavily puddles forming quickly and splashing with the non-stop rain.

Write your own piece of descriptive writing, describing either a school assembly or a fast-food restaurant. Write three paragraphs in response.

Narrative writing

For **GCSE English**, you will need to submit **two** pieces of narrative writing for assessment. One must be a piece of **first-person writing** and the other must be a piece of **third-person writing**.

For **GCSE English Language**, you will be assessed on **one** piece of narrative writing and this can **either** be a first-person narrative **or** a third-person narrative.

The key word to remember when writing a narrative is **control** and also **maturity**. Don't write about haunted houses and anything else far-fetched. Make a decision on what your narrative will be about, and control the length of it by working out the opening and ending before you start writing.

Can you write a sensible narrative?

Look at the student response below. It was written in response to the title 'The school trip'. It is a bright and believable opening.

Student response

"Sit down, Mark. Stop pulling faces out of the window," yelled a very stressed Mrs Peterson. Her eyes were constantly scanning over the seats, checking for any sign of misbehaving. Cheeky glances were exchanged between students. They all looked as if they were planning to hijack the coach.

Imagine that you can fast-forward to the end of the piece of writing above. Can you write the last three sentences of the narrative, to create a sensible and satisfying ending?

EXAMINER'S TIP

- Once you have worked out the ending to your narrative in your head, and have selected the right amount of detail for two or three pages of writing, you will be in a strong position to organize your writing effectively.

Can you write a successful opening and ending?

Openings are important, and endings are also important. Openings provide you with a chance to catch your reader's attention, while a good ending can leave a lasting impression.

The answers that follow were all written in response to the title 'The traitor'.

> **Look closely at each response.**
> - **For each one, discuss the strengths and weaknesses of the opening and ending.**
> - **Discuss how each piece of writing might develop in the middle.**

Student response 1

Opening

Here I am locked away in a cell, with nothing to do but go over what happened again and again in my head. Tomorrow everything will be over. I will be proved innocent as I am going to be put on a stage to answer questions and to be beaten emotionally for everyone to see. How did I get into this mess? It all began on my 19th birthday...

Ending

How I could throw a friendship away like that, I don't know. The moment I hit him I flushed our life away and ruined myself in the process. I realized then, I was the traitor. I am the traitor.

Student response 2

Opening

Auntie Shamie had always said "family morals are the most important thing any family could ask for." Kieron had done the opposite, behind her back. The first time I heard what he was planning to do, I remember thinking it would turn out badly but I didn't say anything to anybody.

Ending

So our lesson was learnt. If ever in doubt, listen to Auntie Shamie. She knew best. Kieron, well he was just "a traitor".

Student response 3

Opening

It was a bright sunny day at college. The students were just coming back from PE. The boys had just returned to get changed. "Where has my phone gone?" Danny asked. "Someone has stolen my phone!" he shouted. He looked through his bag again but there was no sign of it.

Ending

"I can't believe it," Danny thought. "He was supposed to be my best friend," Danny said. "I don't know what to do," he stuttered.

Choose one of the titles below and write an opening and ending for it:

- **On the run**
- **The slide**
- **An unexpected guest.**

Can you organize your writing effectively?

Narrative writing is an account of connected events. A good narrative therefore needs to present what happens in an order that makes sense to the reader. Don't confuse the reader by adding details at the end that you should have mentioned earlier.

The answer below was written in response to the title 'Revenge'.

Student response

I was walking to school with my best friend Neil one morning when this guy came out of his house and started yelling at us about his car. I always walked to school past his house on my way. He shouted at us and said he would make us pay for what we did but we hadn't ever seen him before and we didn't know what he was going on about. He said he was going to wreck something for us to see how we liked it and then went back in his house. We carried on walking our usual walk to school. We'd told him we didn't have a clue what he was talking about but he just went back into the house shaking his head in anger (the car was so badly damaged that it looked like he'd never be able to drive it again – the windows were smashed and it had been burned out).

After school (when I'd got home and had my dinner) he showed up outside. He was standing so I could see him. I was in my bedroom window looking out and I was on my phone talking to Neil about what had happened that morning.

How could you improve the organization of this narrative? Think about how you might rearrange some of the details to make the writing clearer and more interesting.

Organizing your writing is not only a question of how you arrange events. You also need to control your sentences and use paragraphs.

Follow the advice below:

1. Don't let your sentences run out of control. Be conscious of completing each sentence and planting a full stop at the end. Don't use a comma instead of a full stop.
2. Use paragraphs, and make them stand out. Aim to be orderly and neat, so that a page of your writing looks like you intended it to look that way!

The use of sentences in the following piece of writing could be improved. It was written by a student in response to the title 'A day to remember'. Read the response and see what you think.

Student response 1

It's only 11 am the sun is out so bright. My skin is burning even though I walk slowly I feel sweaty. The wind is blowing through. I feel so dirty, thirsty, alone and hot. I can see those little red crabs walking around. I remember my hand swollen up once because I had been grabbed by one and it didn't let go. I'm thinking what the people in the past would do.

> **Make a list of points, suggesting how the answer could be improved. Think about how to divide sentences.**

The next response shows much tighter control. The variety of sentences also helps to add interest to the writing.

Student response 2

I surfaced through the gleaming, shining water. It rippled away as I snorted with laughter. I was holding Jamie's head underwater and my laughter turned to elated glee. Later I sat there, head in hands. Jamie had always hated the water and the horror of being underwater had caused him a lot of pain. I felt so ashamed of myself.

> **What is so effective about the writer's use of sentences in the second response?**

Can you build detail into your writing?

Narrative writing will contain the key features of a story, such as characters and a sequence of events. However, the success of a piece of narrative writing also depends on the quality of your description. Try to be thoughtful about your choice of words and build detail into your writing.

> **Rewrite the following sentences adding extra detail. Change the words to make each sentence more interesting.**
> - **It took me ten minutes to find my phone.**
> - **The road home was dark.**
> - **I felt scared as I walked on to the stage.**

EXAMINER'S TIP

- Don't feel that you need to overload and overcomplicate your sentences in order to make your writing more detailed. Also, avoid dropping impossibly long words into your writing just to impress.

Read the sample writing task below and the student response that follows.

> Write about a time you appeared on stage.

Student response

I could feel my stomach churning. My hands were shaking and I could literally feel my face being drained so that it was chalk white. I knew I could do it though; I was going to be this great big shining star at the end of it. I took a deep breath and thought to myself "after five minutes it will all be over with and everyone will be so proud of you".

> **Discuss with a partner. What is effective about the description in the piece of writing above? What could be improved?**

Can you write with accuracy?

What makes a good, accurate piece of narrative writing? Here is a list of four targets that you should aim for:

1. **Sentences are controlled** – Be aware of how much information you are trying to cram into each sentence. If in doubt, consider breaking things down into separate sentences.
2. **Punctuation is accurate** – Get your full stops right first and remember commas should not be used as full stops.
3. **Spelling is correct** – Know how to spell all simple and regular words. Make sure you know when and where to use apostrophes to avoid silly errors.
4. **Grammar** – Use Standard English, which means avoid slang: you don't have to be posh, just proper!

> **Read each piece of narrative writing below for accuracy. Make a list of corrections for each one.**

Student response 1

I had my notes on what I was going to say until I went in the classy office my heart was thumping even louder i thought I could hear it echo I sat on my desk with my legs over the other in my suit. All of my clients arrived and I introduced myself, looking at there faces they seemd to be so serious. I knew I weren't as nervous anymore

Student response 2

As I lay there, on the small, cold metal bed staring at the bright light as it beams in my eyes, trying to figure out where I was when suddenly several doctors and nurses appear each side of me frantically rushing around me but still oblivious to me. I was willing them to notice me, I was desperate for their help and reassurement but still I had no response, it was hopeless.

Student response 3

I have had my experiences of meeting clowns and one that my family always talk about is when my mum took me shopping up our local town when I was 5 years old and there was a clown right in the middle of the town and I clocked it.

EXAMINER'S TIP

- Get into the habit of checking your work for inaccuracies. Read through your writing quickly at the end of a task, correcting mistakes in spelling, punctuation and grammar. Look out for improperly formed sentences and missing words or letters.

Can you write a personal narrative?

You may have the option to write a personal narrative for your assessment for this unit. Tasks requiring a personal response usually ask you to write about a time when something happened to you, or to write about a person or place that has been important in your life.

Writing a personal narrative is a process of remembering and retelling. It should be written in the first person and should portray events from your perspective.

Many of the same principles apply as when writing any other piece of narrative writing:

- Work out the opening and ending before you write.
- Select the right level of detail to get from your opening to your ending in the time available.
- Organize your writing in paragraphs.
- Control your sentences.
- Write with accurate spelling, punctuation and grammar.

> **Read the responses that appear on the next page. With a partner, discuss the strengths and weaknesses of each opening and ending.**

1 Write about a time when you went to the seaside.

Student response 1

Opening

Our bags were packed and we were ready to hit the open road for our adventure this year. We had sandwiches packed and all that was left was to get into the car, so we could arrive at our destination. Long journey. Great fun...

Ending

...As we got home we were absolutely exhausted. The long journey, the two hours of the younger brother crying and also the breakdown on the motorway: It has been a hectic day and I could hear my bed calling my name. It was time for me to call it a night.

2 Write about a time you were unhappy.

Student response 2

Opening

I felt sad, unhappy; I felt as if I wanted to be alone where no one could bother me. The one person in my life who gave me inspiration had just been taken away from me. My heart felt as if there was a hole, burning, and it was getting bigger...

Ending

...It was now the day of my Grandad's funeral and I looked back at the good times and the bad times and remembered when he was the happiest. After the service I walked out holding my mum's hand, everyone said their bit and it was now mine. I put a rose into the ground and said "I'm going to miss you".

> Write a personal narrative in response to one of the following titles:
> - **Write about a time when you broke something.**
> - **Write about a time when you showed courage.**
> - **Write about a time when you felt you were treated unfairly.**

EXAMINER'S TIP

> - When writing a personal narrative, try to recall descriptive details and even words that were spoken. Try to show what the topic of your writing means to you.

First-person and third-person writing

First-person narratives are written from the point of view of someone in the scene. This means that it is likely to feature the words *I*, *we* and *my*. For example:

Student response

A wonderful day

It was a wonderful day! I was the happiest kid around; my smile was so big it probably could have been seen from miles away. The sun was shining brilliantly in the sky and everything was glowing. Today was the day my life changed forever...

Third-person narratives are written from the point of view of someone who exists outside the story, sometimes close by, sometimes not. Third-person writing therefore uses *he*, *she* and *they* instead of *I*. For example:

Student response

> The crime
>
> It was a late Friday night; he sat at the end of his bed in his clothes. It was a confined room. He slowly stood up in the dark to walk around whilst he thought of what to do.

> **Look back at the examples of first-person narrative writing on pages 148-152.**
> - **How would each piece of writing be different if it was written from a third-person point of view?**
> - **How might this affect the impact of each piece of writing?**

Often when writing third-person narratives for GCSE, students have a tendency to slip into first-person story telling, living the part! Try to avoid doing this. If you start off writing a third-person narrative, stick to it.

In the case of 'The crime', however, the third-person narrative holds right to the end:

> ...He was escorted from the police station to the prison. He was back where he belonged and was told he had to wait for a day in court for another conviction. His mind was blank; he didn't want to think about the days ahead of him.

> **Discuss how the ending above would differ if it was written from a first-person perspective.**

Meanwhile, how did 'A wonderful day' on page 152 end? Not a happy ending, but the first-person narrative held true to the last line:

> *...You never get what you want but that's the reality of life. People say if you wish hard enough your wish will come true. But now I know happy endings only come true in fairy tales.*

It's worth noting, however, that when writing a first-person narrative, you may briefly take on a different perspective, such as a second-person or third-person perspective. A second-person perspective speaks directly to the reader using the word *you*. For example:

Student response

> *You would have been almost knocked unconscious by the sound of his car stereo. It was the loudest thing I've ever heard...*

Likewise, you can even get the suggestion of a third-person description in a first-person narrative. Read the student response on the next page.

Student response

It was a freezing cold December evening in town. I had my warm thermal gloves and my fluffy scarf on. Even though it was cold it was really busy in the town centre, people were walking briskly from shop to shop to try to get away from the crisp cold air. It all started when I saw a man running down the street in front of me. He knocked one woman out of his way before he tripped and fell to the ground next to my feet.

Now look back through this chapter and identify where first-person and third-person writing is used well, in your opinion.

EXAMINER'S TIP

■ If you are writing a first-person narrative, or a piece of first-person descriptive writing, try not to include details that your first-person narrator would not be able to see or be aware of. For example, in the response above, it would not be very convincing if the narrator started telling us about what was going on inside a shop around the corner. From her perspective, in the street, she wouldn't be able to see this in order to tell us about it.

Controlled Assessment Practice – English Language

For GCSE English Language, you will have to write **one** piece of **descriptive writing** and **one** piece of **narrative writing**.

---

1. Write a page of **description** on ONE of the topics listed.
   - Describe the scene in a dining hall or canteen at lunchtime.
   - Describe the scene at a primary school sports day.

2. Choose one of the following options and write a **narrative** of two to three sides.
   - My first party.
   - The rescue.
   - Write about a time when you felt very nervous.

Controlled Assessment Practice – English

For GCSE English, you will have to write **one** piece of **narrative writing** from a **first-person perspective** and **one** piece of narrative writing from a **third-person perspective**.

---

1. Plan and write three paragraphs of **first-person narrative writing** on one of the topics listed below.
   - Write about a time when you had to make a difficult choice.
   - Write about an occasion when you had a narrow escape.

2. Plan and write three paragraphs of **third-person narrative writing** on one of the topics listed below.
   - Taylor's worst day at school.
   - The day Danny discovered the truth.

How is descriptive writing assessed at GCSE?

CONTENT AND ORGANIZATION

Assess your writing using the checklist below to see where you could make improvements.

Content: is it…
- ❑ okay, but patchy?
- ❑ relevant and quite interesting?
- ❑ relevant, makes good sense, and keeps the reader's interest?
- ❑ really well judged and firmly holds the reader's interest?

Organization: is the writing…
- ❑ partly organized?
- ❑ mostly organized?
- ❑ properly organized?
- ❑ really skilfully constructed?

Paragraphs: are they…
- ❑ used?
- ❑ logically ordered and sequenced?
- ❑ used consciously to structure the writing?
- ❑ effective in length and structure to control detail and progression?

Detail: is there…
- ❑ some basic detail?
- ❑ detail that is both realistic and convincing?
- ❑ detail that helps to bring the writing to life?
- ❑ memorable detail that engages the reader?

Vocabulary: is there…
- ❑ a limited range of language with little variation of word choice?
- ❑ some range of language, occasionally selected to create effects?
- ❑ a range of vocabulary selected to create effects or convey precise meaning?
- ❑ a wide range of well-judged, ambitious vocabulary?

How is narrative writing assessed at GCSE?

CONTENT AND ORGANIZATION

Use the checklist below to assess your progress and see where you could improve your writing.

Storyline and characterization: is there…
- ❑ a basic sense of storyline and characters?
- ❑ some control of storyline and characters?
- ❑ overall control of storyline and characters?
- ❑ a well-constructed storyline and developed characters?

Beginnings and endings: is there…
- ❑ a loose sense of a beginning and an ending?
- ❑ a suitable beginning and a well-planned conclusion?
- ❑ a deliberate opening and a satisfactory, meaningful ending?
- ❑ an opening that catches the reader's attention and a thoughtful ending?

Narrative purpose: is it…
- ❑ a simple, basic piece of writing?
- ❑ a narrative with some organization?
- ❑ an organized and purposefully sequenced story?
- ❑ a well-paced, deliberately organized and well-sequenced narrative?

Cohesion: is there…
- ❑ some links between events in the writing?
- ❑ logical connections throughout the narrative?
- ❑ a well thought-out progression of events?
- ❑ a fluid sense of progression from start to finish?

Paragraphs: are they…
- ❑ used?
- ❑ logically ordered and sequenced?
- ❑ used consciously to structure the writing?
- ❑ effective in length and structure to control detail and progression?

Devices: is there…
- ❑ a range of words used appropriately
- ❑ a deliberate choice of vocabulary and a variety of sentence lengths?
- ❑ a deliberate choice of words and sentences to achieve particular effects?
- ❑ a skilful use of words and sentences to achieve effects?

The reader's interest: is the writing…
- ❑ clear enough to follow?
- ❑ clear and believable and developed to hold the reader's interest?
- ❑ controlled, and well shaped, with good pace and detail?
- ❑ developed with originality and imagination; confident and entertaining?

How is the accuracy of your writing assessed?

SENTENCES, SPELLING AND PUNCTUATION

Use the checklist below to check your work and identify how you could improve your accuracy.

Sentences: are they…
- ❏ sometimes used?
- ❏ always used correctly?
- ❏ used correctly and effectively to make meaning clear?
- ❏ used confidently and varied in their length and focus to create effects?

Punctuation: does the writing show…
- ❏ some use of punctuation?
- ❏ accurate use of punctuation including full stops, capital letters and question marks?
- ❏ accurate use of punctuation including full stops, capital letters, question marks and commas?
- ❏ all punctuation used accurately and some use of punctuation to create effects?

Spelling: is the spelling of…
- ❏ simple words usually accurate?
- ❏ simple and regular words usually accurate?
- ❏ simple and regular words correct with some complex words spelt correctly?
- ❏ virtually all words correct including complex and irregular words?

Grammar: is there…
- ❏ rare use of slang and text-message speak?
- ❏ no use of slang and text-message speak?
- ❏ effective use of Standard English throughout?
- ❏ effective use of Standard English throughout and control of tense agreement?

Preparing for Controlled Assessment

Here is the important information from the GCSE specifications for this part of the assessment, including the Assessment Objectives for each specification. The Assessment Objectives show you how you will be awarded marks in your assessment.

GCSE ENGLISH LANGUAGE UNIT 3: Literary Reading and Creative Writing

Using language: creative writing (15%)

Controlled Assessment

You will need to write **one** piece of **descriptive writing** and **one** piece of **narrative writing** based on tasks supplied by the exam board.

AO4 Writing

- **Write to communicate clearly, effectively and imaginatively, using and adapting forms and selecting vocabulary appropriate to task and purpose in ways which engage the reader.**
  This means that you need to make sure that your reader will be able to understand your writing. Keep your sentences crisp and clear. Use your imagination but don't go wild! Make sure your writing is convincing and believable. Pick the right words to help you create a vivid picture in the reader's mind.

- **Organize information and ideas into structured and sequenced sentences, paragraphs and whole texts, using a variety of linguistic and structural features to support cohesion and overall coherence.**
  This means that your writing needs to show a clear sense of direction and purpose. Decide what your opening and ending will be before you start writing. Try to get the level of detail right from the outset. Use controlled sentences and paragraphs to organize your writing.

- **Use a range of sentence structures for clarity, purpose and effect, with accurate punctuation and spelling.**
  This means that your use of sentences needs to be accurate so that your writing makes sense to the reader. You also need to show that you can use punctuation correctly, particularly full stops, commas, question marks, speech marks and apostrophes.

GCSE ENGLISH UNIT 3: English in the World of the Imagination
Writing: open writing (20%), first and third-person narrative

Controlled Assessment

You will need to write **one** piece of **first-person** and **one** piece of **third-person narrative writing** based on tasks supplied by the exam board.

AO3 Writing

- **Write clearly, effectively and imaginatively, using and adapting forms and selecting vocabulary appropriate to task and purpose in ways which engage the reader.**
  This means that you need to make sure that your reader will be able to understand your writing. Keep your sentences crisp and clear. Use your imagination but don't go wild! Make sure your writing is convincing and believable. Pick the right words to help you create a vivid picture in the reader's mind.

- **Organize information and ideas into structured and sequenced sentences, paragraphs and whole texts, using a variety of linguistic and structural features to support cohesion and overall coherence.**
  This means that your writing needs to show a clear sense of direction and purpose. Decide what your opening and ending will be before you start writing. Try to get the level of detail right from the outset. Use controlled sentences and paragraphs to organize your writing.

- **Use a range of sentence structures for clarity, purpose and effect, with accurate punctuation and spelling.**
  This means that your use of sentences needs to be accurate so that your writing makes sense to the reader. You need to use punctuation correctly, particularly full stops, commas, question marks, speech marks and apostrophes.

Check your learning...

Now that you have completed this chapter, rate how well you can perform the following skills on a scale of 1 to 4. '1' means that you still have work to do, while '4' means that you can perform this skill very well.

Can you...

✔ produce creative writing that is believable and engaging?

✔ organize your writing properly?

✔ include the right level of detail in your writing?

✔ choose the right words to say what you mean?

✔ write with accurate spelling, punctuation and grammar?

Your Assessment

This chapter focuses on **transactional writing**, which includes writing texts such as letters, articles, reviews, speeches, leaflets, brochures, factsheets and reports. This chapter also deals with **audience**, **purpose** and **format** and how these factors are likely to influence what you write.

Whether you are studying **GCSE English Language** or **GCSE English** you will need to answer **two** exam questions that will ask you to write two pieces of transactional writing. Each piece of writing will have a different format, purpose and audience.

Learn how to...

✔   write an organized and accurate piece of 'real-life' writing

✔   adapt your writing to suit a particular audience and purpose

✔   write using different formats such as the format of a letter or an article

✔   put opinions across clearly and in an appropriate tone

✔   check your work for accurate spelling, punctuation and grammar.

What is transactional writing?

Transactional writing is 'real-life' writing where writing is produced for a particular audience in order to achieve a particular purpose: for example, a letter to a restaurant manager to complain about bad service or a leaflet persuading young people to volunteer for charity work. This form of writing will also usually involve discussing issues and giving opinions.

The key questions to ask when creating a piece of transactional writing are:
- What is the purpose (i.e. what is the writing trying to do)?
- Who is the audience (i.e. who is the writing aimed at)?
- What is the format (i.e. what is the form and layout of the writing)?

Take a broad topic such as holidays and travel and make a list of possible types of writing that might deal with this topic. For each example, suggest the audience, purpose and format.

Types of text

Here are some examples of the types of text you may be asked to write in your exam:

leaflets

formal reports

speeches

letters

articles

reviews

Formal reports

Formal reports are written to present factual information clearly to the reader. They may be written by one person but they often represent the viewpoints of a number of people. Reports are usually directed at an official leader of an organization; for instance, the chairperson of a governing body.

Features of formal reports include:

- report heading (e.g. 'Report on accidents in PE lessons')
- who the report is for (e.g. 'To head teacher')
- who the report is from (e.g. 'Independent reviewer')
- subheadings (e.g. 'Number of accidents', 'Safety equipment')
- impersonal style (i.e. avoid the use of 'I' – 'The report shows…')
- conclusions/recommendations (i.e. suggestions for future action).

Which of the following situations might require a report?

1. **A resident would like to persuade a leisure centre to provide more facilities for young people.**
2. **A director of a company would like to know how much money is spent on stationery each year.**

Letters

Letter writing is important, even in these days of emails and mobile phones. Formal letters are still used in business and letters from readers are still often printed in newspapers. Informal letters can be sent by snail-mail or email, and should be written in clear and well-organized English.

Features of letters include:

- sender's address in the top right-hand corner
- receiver's name and address on the left-hand side*
- correct opening ('Dear Mrs Smith', 'Dear Editor')
- a number of well-developed paragraphs
- a firm summing-up of the purpose of the letter
- a suitable signing off (e.g. 'Yours faithfully', 'Yours sincerely')*.

Note: Items marked with an asterisk (*) do not apply to informal letters.

Which of the situations below would require a formal letter, and which would require an informal letter? Explain your choices.
1. **A letter of application for a job in a local shop.**
2. **A letter of complaint to a radio station for offensive language.**
3. **A letter to your friend who has recently moved to China.**

Articles

An article is a piece of writing included in a newspaper or magazine. It is not the headline news, but a discussion of a topical issue, often from a particular point of view.

Features of articles include:
- a lively opening to catch the interest of the reader
- a clearly-argued position on the topic being discussed
- an engaging and entertaining written style
- an ending that leaves the reader with something to think about.

When writing an article, you need to choose a **standpoint** on your topic – don't sit on the fence! Take a determined approach to your writing, progressing towards a purposeful conclusion.

The issues mentioned in the activity box below are each worthy of an article. What's your view on each one?

What is your standpoint on each of the issues below? Think of three points to back up your view.
1. **Abolishing school uniforms.**
2. **Banning skating in public places.**
3. **Banning the sale of violent video games in the UK.**

Reviews

Reviews are written to give a personal opinion about things such as TV programmes, films, books, holidays or just about anything you can buy or experience. The aim of the review is to persuade the reader to agree with the writer's opinion.

Reviews should:

- create interest in whatever is being reviewed
- show respect even if the opinion is negative
- steer the reader to a particular point of view
- avoid over-detailed description
- give the important details, such as key features.

What is likely to make a review persuasive? Think about reviews you have read – what usually persuades you?

Speeches

Speeches are usually prepared before they are given. This means that speeches can also be treated as a form of writing. A speech can be formal or informal, depending on who it is aimed at. However, even an informal 'speech' should be written in Standard English.

Guidelines for speeches:

- In most cases, a speech should begin without fuss.
- Write in full sentences because you are arguing a case.
- Notes are not enough – use paragraphs to create a sense of order.
- Usually, you will argue from a personal point of view.

Discuss how the purpose and audience might affect each speech below.
1. **A speech for new starters at your school to prepare them for what they might expect.**
2. **A speech at a charity event persuading people to support a good cause.**
3. **A speech to parents about dealing with bullying.**

Leaflets

Leaflets are usually used to advertise things or to provide information about a particular issue. Often, leaflets can be persuasive, aiming to make the reader think in a certain way.

Features of leaflets include:
- a main heading and subheadings
- bullet points (but not too many)
- columns (sometimes but not always)
- persuasive language, facts and statistics.

Can you write to suit a particular audience and purpose?

Whatever writing task you are given, you will have to write for a particular **audience** and **purpose**. The audience and purpose will affect your writing in a number of ways. For example:
- how you start and finish your writing
- how you structure your points
- the words you choose to use
- how much detail you include
- your tone
- your point of view.

> - **Look at the range of texts that follow and explain the purpose and audience of each one.**

Student response 1

Visit Portugal

A country of sunshine, good food and beautiful sandy beaches; whether you prefer lounging by a pool outside your door or by a beach with the waves lapping at the shore – Portugal is the place to be! Book a trip to Portugal this summer, a friendly welcome awaits you.

Student response 2

Dear Sir/Madam,

My family and I stayed at the sea view apartments as advertised in your brochure for our summer holiday this year. I have to say we were very disappointed with our stay. We do not have a holiday every year and saved up to travel abroad for the first time with our two children.

The apartments turned out to be miles away from the beach and the town. I think the information in your brochure is therefore incorrect and misleading.

Student response 3

Travelling Abroad

You will need to remember:

- Passport: please ensure you check the expiry date of your passport as certain countries will need at least six months remaining.

- Tickets: you will need to show your tickets on arrival at the airport check-in. If you have checked in online prior to arrival, you will need to show a confirmation number.

- Currency: check you have the right currency for the country you are visiting. You can exchange British pounds at high-street banks, travel agencies and post offices.

Student response 4

Eating out in San Melion

If you are looking for a relaxed, yet professional service in a restaurant that caters for all the family in the resort of San Melion, look no further than Pedro's cafe bar in the main street. It doesn't look great from the outside, with many old plastic tables on the sidewalk, but step inside and you will be pleasantly surprised. It is a magical treasure trove of shells, old-fashioned toys and kites, strung in every available space. The staff are very friendly; nothing is too much trouble. The food is a variety of fresh fish, excellent steaks, stews and rice dishes to suit everyone. They will also happily cook something else if you find nothing to your taste.

Can you write a convincing piece of 'real-life' writing?

In the exam, you will have **one hour** to complete two pieces of writing. The situation surrounding the task will be given to you in the exam question, but you may have to build on this using your imagination. Read the sample task below and the student response on the next page.

You have been informed by your local council that a national motorcycle race may be taking place next year in your town. Residents have been invited to write to the council with their views.

Write your letter to the council.

Dear Sir/Madam,

I am writing to you with regards to the motorcycle race which is being planned in the area. As an avid follower of motorcycle racing, I believe it would be a great asset for such an event to be held in the near vicinity. Motorcycle racing can provide sheer excitement and I am sure that the riders who would be attracted would race with tenacity and flair.

This is not a bad start to a letter, clearly signalling what it is about. However, perhaps more could be said about safety to put people's minds at rest.

> **Add another paragraph to the letter, supplying a few more details about the motorbike race.**

Can you write a thoughtful response to a serious topic?

When you are asked to give an opinion, give it – don't sit on the fence. You should be reasonable in the way you argue but it is good to know your standpoint from the outset.

Look at the example task below and read the response on the next page.

> Why are girls more violent these days? Write a speech for a radio phone-in expressing your views.

Student response

> Good afternoon and I'm Becky, I'd like to give my view about 'why are girls more violent these days?' In my opinion, I think it is because times have changed. Around eight years ago they were expected to behave and act properly and men did the work to pay for a living.

The response to this task is not as strong. The thoughts are not very well expressed, and there are some basic, careless errors.

Write your own contribution to the phone-in.

EXAMINER'S TIP

- Even though a radio phone-in could be thought of as an 'informal' form of speech, it should still be written in Standard English. Think carefully about your choice of words and write in controlled sentences.

Write a response to the sample task below.

Technological advances of recent years have brought people together all around the world, but none has done this better than the social networking website Facebook.

Write a magazine article for young people explaining the dangers of Facebook, if used unwisely.

Can you write a lively response to a less serious topic?

Sometimes a task may give you the chance to use humour or add a touch of individual style to your writing. If so, have the confidence to do so!

The opening paragraph below was written in response to a letter-writing task. The student was asked to write to a friend who has recently decided to run the London Marathon.

Student response

Dear Paul,

I am extremely pleased that you have decided to run in the London Marathon and wish you the best of luck. You must have trained hard and become incredibly fit and I am proud of your efforts. I think you are being very brave to run such a huge distance with so many people watching.

There is nothing much wrong with this opening. However, it could perhaps be more lively, entertaining, and even funny. The writer could, for instance, have 'invented' a friend who was unlikely to be suited to running a marathon.

> **See if you can write a more entertaining opening to the letter using your own ideas.**

Can you adapt your style to suit the format?

You will be told what format your writing should take in each exam question. For example, you may be asked to write a letter, an article or the words of a speech. However, it is important that you match the **style** of your writing to the **format** given.

Look back to pages 164 to 167 for the features of each type of writing. You don't need to memorize these features, but you do need to know the differences between these types of writing.

Writing to persuade

Read the student response below. This student was asked to write a **leaflet** persuading people to give up smoking.

Student response

<u>WANT TO STOP SMOKING? WANT TO IMPROVE YOUR LIFESTYLE?</u>

Here at your local health centre, many people come about stopping smoking, but how many of them actually stop?

Smoking is seen to be one of the most unattractive things to do in this day and age. A lot more younger people smoke these days. But why would you want to spend your money on smoking when you could spend it on clothes, or even better save it up?

Since the **purpose** of this leaflet is to **persuade** the reader, it needs more impact. The opening really needs to grab the reader's attention and make it clear why people should give up smoking.

> **How could you give the piece of writing more impact? Discuss your ideas with a partner.**

Writing for or against

The next task asked students to write a **letter** to a local newspaper to give their opinion for or against a smoking ban in public places. Read the task and responses on the next page.

Your local newspaper is running a feature on the ban on smoking in public places in your area and has asked people to write in with their views.

Write a letter to the newspaper for or against the ban on smoking in public places.

Student response 1

> Some people would be positive towards this that banning smoking in public places was the right thing to do, because it harms everyone. But on the other hand other people would be against this because banning smoking in a public place would be pathetic because everyone still does it, yes maybe it harms people but let's face it we're not going to die if someone smokes in public places. It's a public place so the public should have the right to do what they want.

How could the writer make the letter above more effective?

EXAMINER'S TIP

■ Letters need to be written in clear sentences so that the reader can easily follow your argument. Keep your sentences short and direct; stop them before they run on too long and lose their purpose.

The next response is a better example of letter writing. The written style of the opening is much more suited to the letter format.

Student response 2

> Dear Editor,
>
> I am writing to inform you about my opinion concerning the ban on public smoking. I, for one, am supporting this ban. Smokers contribute to secondary smoking whilst they have cigarettes indoors. If they want to smoke, then they should be considerate to the other people in the building and should respect the restrictions of the ban.

■ **Find two things that work well in the letter above.**
■ **Continue the letter adding your own ideas to develop the argument.**

Writing a job application

You cannot possibly have a better excuse for a sense of purpose in your writing than when you apply for a job. Each job is different and that means that you need to have a clear sense of audience too.

Read the following advice from an experienced employer:

I've worked in a high-street recruitment agency for ten years and I have about 30–35 letters and CVs through the post every day. I read them all and try to match the people and CVs to the jobs I have available.

The first thing I notice about a letter of application is whether or not it is clear to read. I also look to see if the skills and personality of the applicant show through in the letter. After the first read, I usually reject about half of the letters. This is often due to the fact that the applicants have not read the job description properly and do not seem to understand the job itself. I then go back through the remaining applications and look for clear evidence that real effort has been made to apply. I check that correct names have been used, and that there is perhaps good evidence of work experience.

Only after all this process do I call and speak to applicants and perhaps five or six will be invited in for a face-to-face interview. This shows that first impressions in the letter really do count. If you do not invest time and energy in the first stage, particularly when you are in a competitive market place, you will not get through to an interview.

Many people are looking for work. You may think you are the best person for the job – then tell me why. Don't expect other people to know this automatically!

> ■ **Read the job description for the General Assistant role on the next page.**
> ■ **Write a letter of application based on the advert, applying for the role offered. Make sure you sell yourself to make sure you would be invited for an interview.**

General Assistant

We require a full-time general assistant for a busy small public relations company. We are a small, local agency looking to recruit a school leaver. You will need to be willing to learn new skills and show an awareness of customer service. You will be answering the telephone, taking messages and dealing with general enquiries. You will be dealing with incoming and outgoing post and a small amount of typing and invoicing. We are prepared to offer ongoing training and an induction package. We are looking for an individual who has a trustworthy, outgoing nature coupled with some IT skills and a willingness to become part of a growing business.

To apply, send an application letter to Office Manager, Wingspan Agency, telling us why you feel you would be suitable for this role. Please ensure you give us your home address and telephone number so we can contact you to arrange an interview if successful. We will reply to all applications.

Check your response against the questions below, adding to your letter if necessary.
- Have you read and understood the job description?
- Have you shown that you are the right person for the job?
- Have you highlighted your key skills and strengths?
- Have you supplied all the information they require?

EXAMINER'S TIP

When writing in the exam, be prepared to make up as much information as necessary, to meet the requirements of the task. If you need to invent examples, then do so.

Writing to engage

You may be asked to write an **article** in your exam. Articles require opinion, argument and persuasion, together with some general knowledge; however, you don't need to be an expert!

When writing an article, you need to start out with a clear position – **for or against**. Like other forms of persuasive writing, you can't write a good article if you are half-hearted about it, you need to commit to your point of view. Look at the example task that follows.

You have been asked to write a lively article for a women's magazine with the title 'How to cope with teenagers'.

Write your article.

- **Read the three openings to the task below and discuss the strengths and weaknesses of each one.**
- **Choose one of the openings to improve. Rewrite it and add at least two further paragraphs.**

Student response 1

Everyone has been a teenager, carefree, grumpy and moody. But as an adult, do you know how to cope with them? Well, this article will show you how.

Student response 2

Yes it can be achieved! Within this article I will tell you how the mind of a teen thinks and how you can live with them. I will tell you the 'golden rule' to whip the untamed beasts into hardworking, 'clean' and healthy human beings. Impossible you say? I think not!

Student response 3

Nowadays, teenagers are judged in such a foolish and unpleasant manner. Why's this? Is it because they hang around in groups and wear hoodies and like to do things differently to others? 80% of people across the UK say they judge teenagers differently.

EXAMINER'S TIP

- Remember that it is always best to open your writing with a focused sentence, rather than a complicated piece of explanation.

Don't be surprised if you are asked to write in a lively or entertaining way. Articles in particular are often written in a range of different styles designed to keep readers interested. You may, for example, decide to adopt a chatty style of writing. However, it is important that you keep this under control. You can use features of spoken English, such as 'well' and 'you know', but don't use them too often.

Similarly, you may choose to add humour to your writing. Again, use it with skill and control. A touch of wit can make a good answer stand out but aiming for side-splitting hilarity is likely to come off badly.

> **Write an article in response to the sample task below. Select a suitable style to reflect the format, purpose and audience given in the task.**

A teenage magazine has invited readers to write a lively article about a well-known person they admire or dislike. You have decided to send in a contribution.

Write your article.

Your article could include:
- an introduction to the person, aimed at your teenage audience;
- the qualities you admire/dislike in this person;
- a conclusion summing up your opinion.

Can you write with accuracy?

Poor spelling, punctuation and grammar spoils a lot of writing at GCSE. In many cases, it is down to carelessness and bad habits, resulting in errors that could be easily avoided.

You must pay attention to your spelling, punctuation and grammar throughout your writing. You need to put effort into targeting weaknesses that you do not want to carry into an exam. While revising the rules below will not guarantee an improvement, they should make you more aware of the key issues surrounding accuracy in writing.

Spelling

- What different rules for **plurals** do you know? Find two errors in the following sentence:

  80% of visitor's go by train but the town also puts on extra busses.

- Is your knowledge of **vowel sounds** and spellings accurate? Correct three errors in the sentence below:

  I recieved your leaflet thruogh the post and would like to voluntear to help.

- Is your spelling of **double consonants** and **consonant clusters** reliable? Find four errors in this sentence:

  If neccessary, I would be willing to demostrate my tallents by preforming one gig for free.

- Are you in command of words with **silent letters**, especially those that begin with them? Rewrite the following sentence correctly:

  Now I no just were you can find the best deals, I dout you will find better anywere!

EXAMINER'S TIP

- Make sure you know the difference between words that sound alike, known as **homophones**. Know when to use each word and which spelling goes with which meaning. For example: *there/their/they're, no/know, here/hear, wear/where.*

Punctuation

Check your written work against the list of top tips below.

- Remember to **stop** at the end of sentences – with full stops, question marks or exclamation marks.
- **Slow down** during sentences or **add pauses** – with commas, brackets and dashes.
- Use semicolons where necessary – such as to link related clauses; **do not** sprinkle them throughout your answer like confetti.
- **Do not** use commas instead of full stops.
- Remember to close **speech marks**.
- Avoid silly errors with **apostrophes** – they are used to mark missing letters or to show that something belongs to somebody or something, for example: *I don't, I can't, Helen's phone, the dog's bowl.*

Grammar

You should avoid using slang and 'text speak' in your writing. Write in Standard English. Make sure you are fully aware of what is regarded as Standard English and what is not. Whatever task you are asked to complete in the exam, you will be assessed on your ability to use Standard English.

> **Put your skills into action by improving the spelling, punctuation and grammar of both pieces of writing below. Make a list of corrections for each one.**

Student response 1

Dear Uncle John and family,

G'day it's Mark from Wales here, How are you?

I just thort I'd write becoz I want to come over to Australia and see you some time in the holidays. Ever since I last come over I want'd to come over again to see the family, I thought of august the something as a date.

Student response 2

We must look after are planet. Rember to switch of lights, and the heating if your warm, else the envirement looses! When you go into a diferent room in you're house switch of the lights before you go. You can also save water. Turn of driping taps and turn the tap of wen you clean you're teath.

Exam Practice

For GCSE English Language and GCSE English you will sit an exam lasting **one** hour in which you must complete **two** transactional or 'real-life' writing tasks. One example task is given below:

> Your school is running an adventure weekend for pupils, offering them the opportunity to stay away from home and take part in activities such as hiking, canoeing and mountain biking.
>
> As head teacher, you are going to write to parents to inform them about the trip.
>
> **Write the letter to parents explaining what the trip will involve, how much it will cost and how pupils might benefit from taking part.**   [20]
>
> Remember to give:
> * information about when and where the trip will take place;
> * an explanation of the activities on offer;
> * details of how children can take part.

Sample answer

Read the response to the task below and the comments on the next page.

Student response

[Recipient's address]   [School address]
                                                                      [Date]

Dear Parents/Guardians,

We are organising a trip for year 6 pupils to Center Parcs.

The planned activities for the trip include nature walks, so your child could learn to love the views and the animals which is what they will see, canoeing, so they will feel the soft warm water on their feet and hands and mountain biking, so they will feel the bumps and lumps of the great outdoors. That is not to mention all the assault courses where they would have fun with their friends.

We arranged this trip for our pupils to give them an experience they probably haven't had. It will be a fun weekend and we hope your child will be able to come along. If you would like your child to come along, then please complete the attached form and please return a cheque for a small fee of £70. This will cover the cost of your child's food, accommodation and to hire the equipment they will need to take part in all of the activities I have mentioned. They may also want to buy sweets for themselves and a gift for you.

We will leave school on Friday 12th June at 3.15pm and we will return on 14th June at 2.00pm. Last year the trip was a great success, so I really hope that your child will be able to come along and take part in this life-changing experience.

Yours faithfully,
Your headmaster
[Signature]

EXAMINER'S COMMENT

This letter has potential but it is let down in places by lapses in style and sentence structure. The opening paragraph, for example, contains some interesting imagery – but is this really what a headmaster would write? The key purpose of this letter is to provide parents with all the information they need to make a decision; however, the details get lost in places.

Although there are certainly some good ideas in this letter, more care could have been taken over language choice. £70 would not be a 'small fee' for most parents and 'life-changing' is perhaps a little extreme. More forward thinking is what is needed here!

How is transactional writing assessed at GCSE?

Assess your writing and find ways to improve it using the checklist below.

Awareness of purpose and format: does the writing show...
- ❑ some awareness of the purpose and format of the task?
- ❑ basic awareness of the purpose and format of the task?
- ❑ clear understanding of the purpose and format of the task?
- ❑ sophisticated understanding of the purpose and format of the task?

Awareness of audience: does the writing show...
- ❑ some awareness of the reader/intended audience?
- ❑ basic awareness of the reader/intended audience?
- ❑ clear awareness of the reader/intended audience?
- ❑ confident awareness of the reader/intended audience?

Content and coverage: does the writing show...
- ❑ some relevant content?
- ❑ a sense of purpose shown in content coverage?
- ❑ a clear sense of purpose shown in content coverage and structure of the content?
- ❑ well-selected, well-judged, and well-organized content coverage?

Ideas and arguments: does the writing show...
- ❑ simple ideas arranged in some order?
- ❑ clear sequencing of ideas giving a sense of an argument?
- ❑ developed and well-sequenced arguments?
- ❑ a sophisticated argument, supported by relevant detail and ideas?

Paragraphs: does the writing show...
- ❑ the use of paragraphs?
- ❑ paragraphs used to show obvious divisions or ideas grouped into some order?
- ❑ logically ordered and sequenced paragraphs?
- ❑ paragraphs used consciously to structure the writing?

Style: does the writing show...
- ❑ some attempt to adapt style to purpose/audience?
- ❑ a clear attempt to adapt style to purpose/audience?
- ❑ a successful and convincing attempt to adapt style to purpose/audience?
- ❑ a confident and sophisticated use of style to suit the purpose/audience?

Vocabulary: does the writing include...
- [ ] a limited range of vocabulary with little variation of word choice for meaning or effect?
- [ ] some range of vocabulary, occasionally selected to convey precise meaning or to create effect?
- [ ] a range of vocabulary selected to convey precise meaning or to create effect?
- [ ] a wide range of appropriate, ambitious vocabulary used to create effect or convey precise meaning?

Sentence structure, punctuation and spelling: is there...
- [ ] some use of sentences?
- [ ] controlled use of sentences?
- [ ] a controlled and varied use of sentences?
- [ ] skilful use of varied sentences to create effect?

Punctuation: does the writing show...
- [ ] some attempt at punctuation?
- [ ] accurate use of punctuation including full stops, question marks and commas?
- [ ] some control of a range of punctuation, including the punctuation of direct speech?
- [ ] a range of punctuation used accurately and effectively to structure sentences and texts?

Spelling: is...
- [ ] the spelling of simple words mostly accurate?
- [ ] the spelling of simple and regular words usually accurate?
- [ ] most spelling, including that of irregular words, usually accurate?
- [ ] virtually all spelling, including that of complex irregular words, correct?

Grammar: is the writing...
- [ ] usually written in Standard English with minor slips?
- [ ] mostly written in Standard English with rare slips?
- [ ] written effectively in Standard English?
- [ ] written effectively in Standard English with some informality used for effect?

Preparing for the exam

Here is the important information from the GCSE specifications for this part of the assessment, including the Assessment Objectives for each specification. The Assessment Objectives show you how your work will be marked.

GCSE ENGLISH LANGUAGE UNIT 2: Using written language

Writing: information and ideas (20%)

Examination

You will need to complete **two** writing tasks testing transactional or 'real-life' writing. Across these tasks you will be asked to write for different audiences and purposes and to adapt your written style to suit the specific format of your writing, for example in letters, articles, leaflets and reviews.

AO4 Writing

- **Write to communicate clearly, effectively and imaginatively, using and adapting forms and selecting vocabulary appropriate to task and purpose in ways which engage the reader.**
  This means that you need to be aware of the audience, purpose and format for your writing. You need to write so that your meaning is clear to the reader. Use your imagination to meet the requirements of the task and to create an interesting and relevant piece of writing. Pick the right words to express yourself precisely.

- **Organize information and ideas into structured and sequenced sentences, paragraphs and whole texts, using a variety of linguistic and structural features to support cohesion and overall coherence.**
  This means that your writing needs to show a clear sense of direction and purpose. Decide what your standpoint will be before you start writing and try to get the level of detail right from the outset. Use controlled sentences and paragraphs to organize your writing.

- **Use a range of sentence structures for clarity, purpose and effect, with accurate punctuation and spelling.**
  This means that your use of sentence structure needs to be accurate so that your writing makes sense to the reader. You also need to show that you can use punctuation correctly, particularly full stops, commas, question marks, speech marks and apostrophes.

GCSE ENGLISH UNIT 2: English in the daily world (writing)

Writing: information and ideas (20%)

Examination

You will need to complete **two** writing tasks testing transactional or 'real-life' writing. Across these tasks you will be asked to write for different audiences and purposes and to adapt your written style to suit the specific format of your writing, for example in letters, articles, leaflets and reviews.

AO3 Writing

- **Write to communicate clearly, effectively and imaginatively, using and adapting forms and selecting vocabulary appropriate to task and purpose in ways which engage the reader.**

  This means that you need to be aware of the audience, purpose and format for your writing. You need to write so that your meaning is clear to the reader. Use your imagination to meet the requirements of the task and to create an interesting and relevant piece of writing. Pick the right words to express yourself precisely.

- **Organize information and ideas into structured and sequenced sentences, paragraphs and whole texts, using a variety of linguistic and structural features to support cohesion and overall coherence.**

  This means that your writing needs to show a clear sense of direction and purpose. Decide what your standpoint will be before you start writing and try to get the level of detail right from the outset. Use controlled sentences and paragraphs to organize your writing.

- **Use a range of sentence structures for clarity, purpose and effect, with accurate punctuation and spelling.**

  This means that your use of sentence structure needs to be accurate so that your writing makes sense to the reader. You also need to show that you can use punctuation correctly, particularly full stops, commas, question marks, speech marks and apostrophes.

Before the day

- Practise keeping control of your work under pressure.
- Be clear about the format and organization of different types of writing.
- Look at lots of transactional writing tasks for problem-solving experience.

On the day

- Read through the tasks at the start of the exam and divide your time equally between them.
- For each of the tasks, decide on your point of view and take stock of the purpose and audience.
- Think through your arguments – be reasonable, but don't sit on the fence!
- Do not waste time drawing pictures or sketching layout features – this is an English exam!

Check your learning...

Now that you have completed this chapter, rate how well you can perform the following skills on a scale of 1 to 4. '1' means that you still have work to do, while '4' means that you can perform this skill very well.

Can you...

✔ produce a piece of writing that is relevant and sensible?

✔ organize your writing properly?

✔ include the right level of detail in your writing?

✔ choose the right words to say what you mean?

✔ write with accurate spelling, punctuation and grammar?

Chapter 3.1

Your Assessment

This chapter focuses on speaking and listening skills and introduces you to how these skills are assessed as part of **GCSE English** and **GCSE English Language**. For this part of your course, you will be assessed in three skill areas:

1. Communicating and adapting language.
2. Interacting and responding.
3. Creating and sustaining roles.

You will complete at least three speaking and listening tasks for assessment. Two of these tasks must have a **real-life context** and one of them must be **based on a literary text**. As part of your work in this unit, you will complete tasks on your own and in groups.

Learn how to...

✔ talk clearly and coherently to others
✔ discuss and listen sensibly within a group
✔ create a convincing role and keep it going.

Speaking and listening effectively

Your teacher will assess your speaking and listening performance based on your overall contribution on the course, which will be underpinned by your work in three different areas, and in at least three different tasks. In other words, you have to earn your marks!

Speaking and listening is at the heart of your course in English or English Language. You have to take part in a wide range of classroom tasks. You have to communicate clearly and you have to show understanding by listening to others and responding to them thoughtfully. Good speaking and listening skills are essential for success in the world outside the classroom and learning to listen and communicate effectively will help you to improve your work in other areas of the course too.

Take stock of your skills

How will you improve your speaking and listening mark? It's no good forever saying that you lack confidence or you don't like drama. Nobody is expecting you to audition for a starring role in the next reality TV show!

But you do need to recognize and do something about your weaknesses. This is the sure way to stretch yourself to get the marks you are capable of.

> ■ **Discuss the statements below and give tips and hints for each one.**
> ■ **Write your own statement explaining what you find most challenging about speaking and listening.**

My teacher says I should have prepared more, and I should say things that are more relevant to the topic. I suppose I need to think before speaking.

I get frustrated when other people are slow or don't take the point that I'm making seriously.

I need to take into account what other people say. I need to listen more.

I get ideas in my head but can't put them into words. I'm not quick enough and I start to mumble.

I'm not sure how to give a talk. I get really nervous and go blank.

I don't want people to switch off and look bored. I want to do well, but last time I read something out badly and it was terrible.

EXAMINER'S TIP

■ When you give a talk, make sure you have a clear sense of your purpose and audience. Choose your content and your tone to appeal to the people you are speaking to. Make sure your talk is the right length and includes the correct level of detail.

Can you explain yourself clearly in sentences?

A sentence is not the same in speech as it is in writing, but it is a handy term to use. If you use a string of words that make sense to a listener, that will do. Sometimes it is OK to answer with a single word or a short phrase, but clear sentences are really needed to deliver good sense.

> **Explain that you were late for your lesson because you were asked to take a visitor to the other side of the school.**

When explaining things it usually makes sense to adopt a fairly neutral tone so that you can put all the facts across clearly to the listener. **Don't** say:

> It wasn't my fault I'm late, so why are you blaming me?!

Can you ask questions clearly to help solve a problem?

Asking questions is a natural part of problem solving. You ask questions to get more information, so you can take all factors into account when making a decision.

> **There is a visitor standing outside your classroom before a lesson. She looks completely lost and a little stressed. What questions would you ask in order to help her?**

To seek and obtain information effectively you need to listen and be perceptive. People may not always give you the information you need straight away, so you may need to ask different questions and try different approaches. **Don't** say:

> Are you the supply for Tommo? The last one ran away, you know!

Can you talk about a complex topic?

It's time to get your ideas in order and speak out! Sometimes it may seem easier to do nothing rather than be successful in speaking and listening. Frankly, lots of people lack confidence, but that is no excuse for being a lazy thinker.

- Consider the questions in the coloured strips below, and work out a thoughtful answer to each one.
- Discuss the questions in pairs, working towards agreement.
- If you can't reach complete agreement, break down your views even further and work out which points you agree on and where you disagree.

Are you proud to live in Britain?

Should you always respect your elders?

Should verbal abuse be punished as a crime?

Can your sense of humour be explained?

What is a supplementary question?

A **supplementary question** is a question that comes from the discussion of the main question that you are focusing on. It normally takes the discussion into greater detail in some way. In a situation like a TV interview, the professional interviewer will always be ready with another question in order to move the discussion forward. For example: 'Can you be proud to live in Britain without being arrogant?' 'Should you respect your elders even if they behave unfairly?'

For each of the questions in the coloured strips above, think of supplementary questions that would move each discussion along.

Can you give a reasoned opinion?

Opinion is free. Within reason, you can have whatever opinion you want on a subject, but it will help you in the real world to have a few open-minded views. At the very least, you need to know that not everybody will agree with you!

Give constructive reasons for your opinions. **Don't** say:

I just hate it 'cos it's stupid!

> **In pairs, choose a current news, sports or entertainment topic that you both have an opinion on.**
> - **Take it in turns to explain your opinion and give reasons.**
> - **Explain why you agree or disagree with your partner's view.**

The best speaking and listening work has a clear sense of **audience** and **purpose**. This applies to giving your opinion on a topic. When giving your point of view, the purpose will generally be to convince the listener to agree with you. However, you are more likely to make a convincing argument if you take into account opposing points of view and try to respond to them.

Consider the following topics:

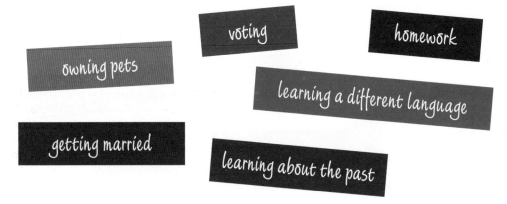

> **In pairs:**
> - **think of arguments in favour of and against the topics above**
> - **decide what your opinion is in each case**
> - **think of more topics that get people talking.**

EXAMINER'S TIP

Here are some sure-fire tips for success in speaking and listening work:
- put your points across clearly
- use Standard English
- adapt your style to suit different situations and different personalities
- listen with concentration to the teacher and fellow students
- support and respect others
- ask relevant questions.

Can you work with others in a group?

You are likely to work with different groups of students throughout the course and the number of people in each group will vary. Working with a partner is regarded as group work, but it is very different from working with a team of five or six people.

Read the following guidance for working with someone you know in a pair:

> Students are generally comfortable when asked to do a task with a friend. They do not always see it as work, because the company is enjoyable. If they are focused, both students are fulfilled and learn something.

Think through the different situations below and write guidance for each one. Advise other students about how to get the most out of working in each type of group.

- two random people put together as a pair
- three people working together
- four people working together
- two pairs of friends put together to compare ideas
- more than four people in a group

Can you give constructive feedback to others?

Sometimes you need someone you trust to tell you the truth. For this reason it may be useful to work with a partner, even when you are preparing an individual speech or contribution. In these situations, ask your partner to observe and listen to you as you speak and provide honest feedback at the end.

In return for this, you should pay extra close attention when your partner is speaking. Note what he or she does well, as well as listing points for improvement. Success in speaking and listening has a lot to do with confidence so hearing positive feedback can be really helpful.

Some of the following comments may be relevant, but you might think of others. Be fair, but firm.

> You look down at the floor too much; try to make better eye contact with your audience.

> You sometimes introduce too many ideas all at once, without developing them properly.

> You don't always have to try to be funny – you can be serious sometimes too.

> You pretend you're shy, but you're not.

> Sometimes you speak over people – make sure you take time to listen to others.

> You speak too quickly – try to slow it down.

Set some targets for your partner. Give him/her tips about how to improve. Check back on these later in the course.

EXAMINER'S TIP

- Remember to listen carefully and sympathetically in a discussion. When it's your turn to speak, use what you have heard to give specific responses to what others have said.

Speaking and listening tasks for every occasion

You may be asked by your teacher to do any number of the tasks from the following pages. All of them require a little thought and planning, but none of them requires a huge amount of research or expert knowledge.

Communicating and adapting language

In all of the following examples, the focus is on making a **clear individual contribution**. If you give a talk, it should last around five minutes, with possible extra time at the end for you to answer questions from your audience.

Give an account of a personal experience

Even though this task is straightforward, you will need to do some preparation. Using notes is allowed here, but you should avoid relying on too many of them. Reading your 'story' is not acceptable.

> **Choose one of the following:**
> - **Talk about a time when you battled to get something done.**
> - **Talk about an experience that shocked you.**
> - **Talk about a time when you had a narrow escape.**

The sense of purpose in any of the above will come from reflecting upon the lessons you learned from the experience and the advice you might pass on to others.

Present an argument for or against a local issue

In this kind of task, you should think about how the issue in question might affect people in your community. Decide what your personal point of view is on the topic and make a speech, trying to persuade your audience to agree with you.

> **Choose one of the following:**
> - **Talk about vandalism and graffiti in your area, including problems and solutions.**
> - **What could be done to improve the environment in your area?**
> - **Talk about a risk to young children where you live and what could be done to improve their safety.**

Give a talk on a challenging topic

In this task, planning and preparation are highly important. You will be giving an opinion but this must be backed up with good, factual reasons that reflect your knowledge and understanding.

> **Choose one of the following:**
> - **Films are more appealing to young people than books. What is your opinion?**
> - **'Money alone can't make you happy.' Discuss.**
> - **Are violent computer games bad for society?**

Give a talk on a literary text

You will need to have good knowledge of your set text to talk about it confidently and in detail, but as with any speaking and listening task, you also need to pay attention to your **audience** and **purpose**. Are you giving a talk to people who have also studied the text? If so, don't waste time re-telling the story. Is your purpose to give your opinions about the text or to raise awareness of a particular issue?

There are many possible approaches to this type of task and it is easy to get lost and waffle on. The key is to plan your talk with a clear approach in mind and to stick to it during your presentation!

> **Choose one of the following:**
> - **Who is the most important character in the text and why?**
> - **What is the most important issue raised by the text and why?**
> - **What do you think the writer wanted to achieve by writing the text?**

How are individual presentations assessed?

Use the following checklist to assess your performance in speaking and listening and to work out where you could make improvements.

Communicating: did you...

- ❑ briefly give your point of view, ideas and feelings?
- ❑ give straightforward but extended ideas and explanation?
- ❑ raise issues and points of view effectively?
- ❑ interpret information, ideas, feelings and points of view confidently?
- ❑ highlight and prioritize the important details of a complex subject-matter?

Adapting: did you...

- ❑ sometimes supply detail to add interest?
- ❑ begin to adapt your talk and non-verbal features for different audiences?
- ❑ adapt your talk and non-verbal features to a variety of situations and audiences?
- ❑ confidently adapt and shape your talk and non-verbal features to meet different demands?
- ❑ use a sophisticated range of strategies to deal effectively with challenging situations?

Standard English: did you...

- ❑ use straightforward vocabulary and grammar, with some features of Standard English?
- ❑ use a variety of vocabulary, with accurate Standard English?
- ❑ use a range of well-judged vocabulary and sentence structures for different purposes, with accurate Standard English?
- ❑ make appropriate, controlled and effective use of Standard English vocabulary and grammar?
- ❑ show skilful and flexible use of Standard English vocabulary and grammar?

Interacting and responding

In the following tasks the focus is for you to **work as part of a team** (a pair or a small group). Remember that listening skills are just as important as speaking skills. The aim of the tasks is to come to some kind of agreement through taking part in a reasoned discussion.

Discussion of a familiar topic

A 'familiar topic' is something that is likely to affect your everyday life and, therefore, is likely to be something that you have a clear opinion about. You should, however, try to develop your views sensibly and seriously as you listen to others.

Choose one of the following:

- **Celebrities are often the focus of the news these days; do you think this is a good or bad thing?**
- **What impact would not having a mobile phone have on your everyday life?**
- **Do you think there is any need for school uniforms these days?**
- **Should parents encourage their children to support the same football team as they do?**

EXAMINER'S TIP

- When taking part in a group discussion, make sure you concentrate hard on the task, speak confidently and interact with the student(s) you are working with.

Discussion of a less familiar topic

You may be asked to take part in a discussion on a topic that you do not spend much time thinking about on a day-to-day basis. However, it is still likely to be something that you are able to form an opinion on. Try to back up your opinions with thoughtful reasoning.

Choose one of the following:
- **'The world would be better without cars.' Discuss this view.**
- **It should be compulsory for everybody to learn life-saving first aid. Develop your views.**
- **Sending criminals to prison is a useless form of punishment. What do you think?**

Discussion based on a set text

The focus of this type of task is to provide a personal response to the study of literature. Working with other students is an excellent way to firm up your ideas in your mind and to develop them in more detail. Be prepared to listen carefully to other people's views and move the discussion forward by asking questions and making comments.

DISCUSSION OF UNSEEN POETRY

Work in pairs to discuss unseen poems from past GCSE English Literature papers or poems provided by your teacher. In the exam, you will have to respond to unseen poems on your own, but working as a pair is good practice in 'thinking skills'.

- **What is the 'voice' or the point of view expressed in the poem? What is the situation at the start of the poem?**
- **Switch your attention to the ending of the poem and discuss the last comment or sentence offered by the poet. What might the poet be trying to say?**
- **Discuss several poems of different styles and structures, and compare your ideas with other pairs. This speaking and listening task will also help you to gain confidence when writing about poetry.**

How are group discussions assessed?

Use the following checklist to assess your performance in speaking and listening and to work out where you could make improvements.

Interacting: did you...

❑ follow the main ideas and raise straightforward questions?
❑ allow others to put their views across and respond appropriately?
❑ show that you appreciate feelings and ideas expressed by others, recognizing obvious bias or prejudice?
❑ make progress towards a useful outcome in each situation and help to structure the discussion with your contributions?
❑ start off, develop and carry on discussion through encouraging others to participate, sorting out differences and moving towards a positive outcome?

Responding: did you...

❑ respond to what you heard, showing some interest and understanding?
❑ respond positively to what you heard, making helpful requests for further detail?
❑ listen closely and attentively, showing clear understanding of what you heard?
❑ challenge, develop and respond to what you heard in thoughtful and considerate ways?
❑ remain a sensitive and active listener throughout, showing understanding of complex ideas?

Contributions: did you...

❑ make brief, occasional contributions and general statements in discussion?
❑ make specific, relevant contributions to discussion?
❑ make significant contributions that moved discussions forward?
❑ reflect on ideas expressed by others, asking questions to clarify issues and to develop the discussion?
❑ shape the direction and content of the talk, developing and challenging ideas?

Creating and sustaining roles

The speaking and listening tasks that follow all require you to **take on a role**. This means you must speak and act as if you are yourself or somebody else in a specific situation. You will be allowed to improvise and adapt your role on the day, but preparation in advance will boost your confidence.

Create a role in a familiar situation

For your assessment, you may be asked to take part in a role-play that is based on a familiar situation, such as situations that you are likely to face at home and at school in everyday life.

Choose one of the following:

■ **You purchased a set of headphones from a high-street store in the January sale, but after a couple of days they stopped working. The store does not normally offer refunds on sale items. How will you deal with the problem?**

■ **You are a skilful drummer who practises regularly. However, a new neighbour has moved in next door and has complained about the noise. How are you going to resolve the situation?**

■ **You need to ask your parents to pick you up from a friend's party. However, you know they already have plans that night. How are you going to persuade your parents to help?**

> **EXAMINER'S TIP**
>
> ■ When taking part in a role-play, prepare properly by making sure you understand your role. Think in advance about how you would be likely to feel and behave if you were actually in the situation. Make sure you are clear on the point of view of the person you are playing.

Develop and sustain a role in a less familiar situation

You may be asked to take on a role in a less familiar situation, such as in a shop or an office environment. These are likely to be community-based situations, but you may be asked to play the role of somebody other than yourself. Make sure you use appropriate language, tone and grammar to suit the situation. Plan the conversation in advance to ensure you get a positive outcome.

Choose one of the following:

- You work at the box office of a cinema. A family of two adults and three teenagers would like to buy tickets for a film rated 15, but at least two of the teenagers do not look old enough. You have to ask them for ID or refuse them entry. How do you do this without upsetting them?

- You are an attendant at a theme park and you have noticed two people who keep jumping over barriers in order to push to the front of the queue. Other people in the queue have noticed and are getting annoyed. How do you deal with this without causing a confrontation?

- You are an attendant at a busy railway station. All trains to Manchester have been severely delayed due to bad weather. A lot of passengers have no choice but to wait for the next train. Many of them are worried and annoyed. How do you deal with the situation?

Participating in a radio phone-in

Phone-ins are now a daily feature of radio and TV. Football phone-ins, for example, are particularly popular. The focus of most football phone-ins is to allow fans to call up after a match and discuss their team's performance. Radio presenters will usually ask questions to prompt discussion.

Listen to a live broadcast or a recording of a radio phone-in for football supporters. How do the callers speak and interact with the presenter and other callers?

The role-play activity on the next page requires you to set up your own phone-in. This activity is based on football, but phone-ins may deal with other issues of interest. When setting up this kind of role-play, keep in mind that communication typically takes place over the phone. Think about how this is likely to affect what you say and do.

SET UP YOUR OWN FOOTBALL PHONE-IN
Have two 'presenters' at the front of the class ready to receive calls in an authentic manner from 'members of the public'. Some of the class can be lined up to make the 'calls', while others can form the 'audience' who can listen to the calls and give their opinions on the relevance and quality of each contribution.

For the task above to work effectively, you may need to spend a little time familiarizing yourself with football-related topics. The 'callers' also need to appreciate that the presenter (or producer) can cut them off at any time.

Convincing a panel of judges

Another form of discussion that has become a popular source of entertainment is the individual versus the panel of judges. Do you like seeing people make a spectacle of themselves on TV? Then watch an episode of *The Apprentice* or *Dragons' Den*! These TV programmes capture the actions and reactions of people as they try to reason with a panel of experts.

In the TV programme *Dragons' Den*, people who think they have a good business idea try to persuade multi-millionaires to invest in them. The trouble is that some of the ideas are hopeless! Another problem is that some of the applicants lack the persuasive skills to convince the investors to part with their money.

Watch one of the programmes mentioned above or another programme featuring a speaker and a panel of judges. Make two lists:
1. Things that people do wrong.
2. Things they say that impress the panel.

In the real world, panels are used in all kinds of situations from hearing a sales pitch, to university applications, to job interviews.

In groups of four, put together your own panel interview for the job described on the next page. The panel should be made of three representatives from the company and the fourth person should play the role of the applicant. Take it in turns to apply, with the aim of convincing the panel to hire you. At the end of the activity, take a vote on who should get the job – you can't vote for yourself!

Car Sales Executive

We are currently looking to recruit a car sales executive to join our busy team. The ideal candidate will have excellent communication skills and be highly self-motivated. You should be well organized and have experience of working with the public on a face-to-face basis. You must be dynamic and able to adapt to new processes and be enthusiastic about selling in a target-driven and competitive environment.

Create an improvisation based on a literary text

At least one of the tasks you will be assessed on for your speaking and listening assessment will be based on a literary text you have studied. You may, for example, take part in a role-play where you play the part of one of the **characters**. Alternatively, you could play the part of a **person connected with the text** such as the writer discussing his/her aims, or a director putting forward a pitch for a film adaptation.

Choose one of the following:

■ **With a partner, improvise a dialogue between two characters from one of your set texts. The dialogue should take place after the main events of the story and should look back on what has happened.**

■ **You are an upcoming film director. You would like to make a new film adaptation of the text you have studied and you are going to pitch your ideas to a panel of three representatives from a film company. The representatives should ask questions and weigh up their opinions before deciding whether or not they would like to back the production.**

Your response to this kind of task should not be scripted, but a short planning session is in order to think through the content of the improvisation and to develop a clear sense of your chosen role.

How is role-play assessed?

Use the following checklist to assess your performance in speaking and listening and to work out where you could make improvements.

Creating: did you...

- ❏ draw upon ideas to create a simple character?
- ❏ create a straightforward character using speech and movement?
- ❏ sustain a role through appropriate use of language and effective movement?
- ❏ create a convincing character role using a range of techniques?
- ❏ create a complex, challenging character through a range of dramatic approaches?

Sustaining: did you...

- ❏ react to situations showing some understanding of relationships and familiar ideas?
- ❏ become involved with situations, showing understanding of issues and relationships?
- ❏ help to develop situations and ideas, showing understanding of relationships and significant issues?
- ❏ respond skilfully and sensitively to explore ideas, issues and relationships?
- ❏ explore and respond to complex ideas, issues and relationships?

EXAMINER'S TIP

- When working in role, remember to speak and act like the character throughout. If you go back to just speaking as yourself, you will lose marks.

Preparing for the speaking and listening Assessment

Here are the important details from the GCSE specifications for this part of your course, including the Assessment Objectives, which show you how your skills will be assessed.

GCSE ENGLISH LANGUAGE UNIT 4: Spoken Language

Using language (20%)

Assessment

You will be required to complete at least **three** speaking and listening tasks and at least two of these tasks must be based on a 'real-life' situation. At least one of the tasks must be based on a literary text you have studied. You will be assessed on your ability to use your speaking and listening skills to explore ideas, texts and issues through scripted and improvised work.

The three tasks will cover the following areas:
- Communicating and adapting language
- Interacting and responding
- Creating and sustaining roles.

AO1 Speaking and Listening

- **Speak to communicate clearly and purposefully; structure and sustain talk, adapting it to different situations and audiences; use Standard English and a variety of techniques as appropriate.**
  This means that you are able to change your speech to match the task and to make sure that your listeners can understand you. You will be assessed on your ability to use Standard English effectively.

- **Listen and respond to speakers' ideas, perspectives and how they construct and express their meanings.**
  This means that you need to show that you can listen to others. You need to take on board other people's ideas and help them to develop them, appreciating the fact that different people often have different views.

- **Interact with others, shaping meanings through suggestions, comments and questions and drawing ideas together.**
  Good listening is shown through interaction. You need to show that you can use a range of techniques, such as asking questions and making comments to help maximize and shape the involvement of others.

- **Create and sustain different roles.**
  This means that you need to be able to think and speak from the point of view of somebody else in a specific situation. This could be a 'real-life' scenario, or it could be based on characters from a text you are studying.

GCSE ENGLISH UNIT 4: Speaking and Listening
Speaking and Listening (20%)

Assessment

You will be required to complete at least **three** speaking and listening tasks and at least two of these tasks must be based on a 'real-life' situation. At least one of the tasks must be based on a literary text you have studied. You will be assessed on your ability to use your speaking and listening skills to explore ideas, texts and issues through scripted and improvised work.

The three tasks will cover the following areas:
- Communicating and adapting language
- Interacting and responding
- Creating and sustaining roles.

AO1 Speaking and Listening

- **Speak to communicate clearly and purposefully; structure and sustain talk, adapting it to different situations and audiences; use Standard English and a variety of techniques as appropriate.**
  This means that you are able to change your speech to match the task and to make sure that your listeners can understand you. You will be assessed on your ability to use Standard English effectively.

- **Listen and respond to speakers' ideas, perspectives and how they construct and express their meanings.**
  This means that you need to show that you can listen to others. You need to take on board other people's ideas and help them to develop them, appreciating the fact that different people often have different views.

- **Interact with others, shaping meanings through suggestions, comments and questions and drawing ideas together.**
  Good listening is shown through interaction. You need to show that you can use a range of techniques, such as asking questions and making comments to help maximize and shape the involvement of others.

- **Create and sustain different roles.**
  This means that you need to be able to think and speak from the point of view of somebody else in a specific situation. This could be a 'real-life' scenario, or it could be based on characters from a text you are studying.

How to be a good speaker

- Do not stray from the topic being discussed.
- Do not repeat points that have already been made, unless you have something new to add.
- Make eye contact with your audience; do not stare at the floor or out of the window.
- If you are making a short comment, rehearse it in your mind before saying it aloud. Also, your first sentence of a longer speech should be clear and direct.
- Always try to make at least one relevant point in a discussion.
- If you are nervous, try to get a comment in early.
- Do not interrupt other speakers. In discussion, it is a matter of judgment when to speak.
- Vary the tone of your voice; do not speak in a monotone.
- Do not take over a discussion; make sure you allow others to speak.
- Be enthusiastic (or at least positive) about the topic or task.
- When you talk to an audience, make sure that your body language is positive; do not lean or slouch.
- Do not place your hand over your mouth when speaking.

How to be a good listener

- Always be involved in discussions, even if you are just listening carefully to what is being said.
- Do not yawn or look bored.
- When listening to a speaker, face them and give them your full attention.
- Be aware of your body language; you should look as if you are listening, for instance, by leaning forward and concentrating.
- Encourage other, nervous speakers with an occasional nod and smile.

Tips for interacting with your audience

- When giving a talk, vary the way you communicate with your audience – for example consider using visual aids or building multimedia elements into your presentation.
- If the topic of your talk allows it, consider including a practical demonstration (for example: applying make-up to a model; coaching a particular skill).
- Consider using a seating plan or changing the location of your talk (for example: a computer room, gym or lecture hall).
- Using rhetorical questions can make your listeners think, but if you really want to keep the members of your audience on their toes, you could consider asking one or two of them a direct question.
- If you choose to use 'direct questioning', use it sparingly to help illustrate a point.
- Keep your questions short and simple and ensure you are fairly confident about what the other person will say. For example: 'How many people do you think fail their driving test each year? I can tell you that the answer actually is…'
- Encourage your audience to ask questions at the end of your presentation. Think about the kind of questions that are likely to come up in advance, so that you can offer a well-thought-out response.

Check your learning...

Now that you have reached the end of this chapter, rate your performance in speaking and listening by giving yourself a score of 1 to 4 for each skill listed below. '1' means that you still have work to do, while '4' means that you can perform this skill very well.

Can you...

✔ speak clearly and effectively in Standard English?

✔ listen with attention and make thoughtful contributions to discussions?

✔ keep a role going with purpose?

Your Assessment

This chapter introduces you to the study of spoken language, which is likely to be new to you at GCSE. Studying spoken language is tested by Controlled Assessment. For this, you will have to write an essay focusing on how spoken language is used, either by yourself or other people.

Learn how to...

✔ recognize the different features of spoken English

✔ study spoken language fairly closely and make meaningful, detailed comments on it

✔ use some of your own speaking and listening experience to show your understanding of spoken language

✔ show how spoken language changes in different contexts

✔ understand how spoken language changes for different listeners

✔ recognize standard and non-standard forms of spoken language

✔ successfully write an essay of three or more pages on a study of spoken language.

What is spoken language?

Spoken language is around us all the time; it is the speech that we hear or utter every day. Here are some examples:

ordering in a restaurant

asking for something in a shop

watching a TV programme

listening to a radio programme

talking to friends or family members

What other examples of spoken language can you think of?

Differences between writing and speech

The main difference between spoken and written language is obvious – one is heard and the other is read! But there are other important differences too. For example, when using written language, you write in sentences and use full stops, commas, question marks and exclamation marks. When using spoken language, you can use pauses, volume (loud or quiet) and the **way** you say words instead.

Can you think of other differences between spoken English and written English?

Features of spoken English

When speaking naturally, people often use words or sounds to fill pauses. These are called **fillers**. The piece of speech below includes many examples!

> It's ...so like... weird... sort of ...when... you... like... talk... cos like you say like... like what I just did... so yeah ...it's kind of weird and stuff ...and things like that... if you get what I mean ...yeah... you know like...

> **Have a conversation with a partner in which you contribute a sentence each – with no more than one filler per sentence. Like a tennis match – the ball is allowed to bounce only once!**

Interruptions, pauses and turn-taking are other familiar features of conversation. Someone may **interrupt** what another person is saying for different reasons, such as needing to say something urgently, or if they are just being rude.

> **What reasons do people have for pausing in their speech?**

Turn-taking should be straightforward in a conversation between two people, but does each person always say the same amount? Think about your own experiences.

> **What happens to turn-taking when there are three or four people in a group? What happens in bigger groups?**

Recognizing different features of spoken English

When writing about spoken language, you should write about anything you find interesting about it. Don't be put off by feeling you have to look for complicated technical features. You are writing about the language you use every day!

The activity box below, however, covers some features of spoken language that you may choose to write about in your assessment.

> **Find examples of each of the following features of spoken English in the speech bubble below:**
>
> - **unfinished sentences**
> - **pauses**
> - **repeated words or phrases**
> - **fillers (words or sounds filling a pause)**
> - **contractions (shortened forms of words)**
> - **informal words**
> - **tag questions (questions that come at the end of a sentence).**

Well, I'm... I'm not sure I can help you, I could help if I ...er... had a bit more ready cash... and... you should've given me some notice really shouldn't you? I mean I mean I would've liked to have helped but...

EXAMINER'S TIP

- Be selective about commenting on features of speech. Look for trends in the way somebody speaks. You don't have to comment on every single 'filler' any more than you need to comment on every comma in a novel!

Spoken language in different forms

The two main forms of spoken language are spontaneous speech and scripted speech. **Spontaneous spoken language** is unscripted speech; for example, speech that people use in everyday life when talking to friends or family. An example of **scripted spoken language** is a formal presentation, such as a speech by a representative from a company.

In your Controlled Assessment, you are likely to base your response on a transcript of spontaneous speech but you may also use evidence from different forms of spoken language. Read the descriptions below and think about the questions that follow each one.

Transcripts: A transcript is a written version of a recording of spoken language. It tries to show the features of spoken English that are different from standard written English, such as pauses and fillers.

> **What do you think is useful about having a transcript of a speech? Why could it be difficult to create a transcript?**

Recordings: These could be audio only (something you listen to; for example, a radio programme), or audio-visual (something you listen to and watch; for example, a TV programme).

> **What do you think are the advantages of using recordings when studying spoken language? What are the disadvantages?**

Recollections: Recollections are memories – in this case, memories of the way spoken language has been used that relates to a topic you are researching.

> **How could you use recollections of speech? What problems are connected with recollections?**

Working with transcripts

You won't have to create a transcript, but you are likely to work with one as part of your study of spoken language. A transcript can be backed up by watching a video recording. This may allow you to make comments about other features of communication, such as eye-contact, body language and hand gestures. Any of these features might be key to a speaker's 'performance'. The recording, in other words, brings the transcript to life.

Look at the transcript below with a partner. It is the words of a discussion in which a young man is asked to account for his behaviour in the community.

Rachel	He told me that he's seen you almost every night this week, with your hood up…
Lloyd	So what, I ain't done nothing to him.
Rachel	…looking extremely intimidating
Alex	Actually, you intimidate, you and your gang.
Lloyd	Nah, I haven't touched you, I haven't touched anything, I haven't said nothing.
Alex	Well how come, my children and my wife are afraid to leave the house in the evenings because they've seen gangs like you and they're scared of you, there's no other word for it.
Lloyd	Cos you're just fools.
Alex	Just fools…
Lloyd	exactly, you just stay in the house like wimps bro.. Yeah you just stay away, just stay away…
David	There seems to be a real breakdown of communication here, I mean have you two ever met before?
Rachel	He's just trying to get his point across…
Alex	No I am just trying to…
Lloyd	*[interrupts]* Nah he's just shouting, just shouting.
Alex	No, I am trying to make you understand that the way you act in our area is disgraceful because I have neighbours, elderly women, who won't leave the house unless you're in school, unless gangs like yours are definitely off the streets.
Lloyd	That's the problem. I haven't said they can't come out. I ain't said…

> **With a partner, make notes on any points of interest in the transcript above. How accurately do you think it represents real speech? How is each person behaving? What do you learn about each of them?**

Studying scripted speech

Most speeches by politicians and other professional speakers are scripted. They are learned and read or performed using an autocue. They are often not written by the speaker. Here, for example, is part of President Obama's inauguration speech:

> For everywhere we look, there is work to be done. The state of the economy calls for action, bold and swift, and we will act – not only to create new jobs, but to lay a new foundation for growth. We will build the roads and bridges, the electric grids and digital lines that feed our commerce and bind us together. We will restore science to its rightful place, and wield technology's wonders to raise health care's quality and lower its cost. We will harness the sun and the winds and the soil to fuel our cars and run our factories. And we will transform our schools and colleges and universities to meet the demands of a new age. All this we can do. And all this we will do.

What are the differences between this transcript and the one in the activity on the previous page? What features of this transcript show that it is scripted?

For light relief, rewrite the extract from the speech above adding in your own fillers to your heart's content. President Obama would probably enjoy it . . .

Writing about spoken language

Although you may not have studied spoken language before, it is not so different to other areas of your English Language course. A bit of practice will help you learn what to look for and comment on when writing about spoken language.

Here are some sentences from students' essays just to show the kinds of things that could be said about spoken English:

There are examples which show us that this is spontaneous speech, for example, the repeated pauses in the middle of sentences...

There are examples of informal speech that show this person might be talking to someone they know, such as "Alright, mate?" and "Cheers".

The use of fillers such as "erm..." helps to show that the texts are spoken language.

> **Practise writing about spoken language. Write three or four paragraphs on a presentation, a role-play or a discussion from the classroom. Remember to:**
> 1. **Make comments on the way people speak, especially things such as the person's volume, pace and body language.**
> 2. **Make detailed comments on the words and sentences spoken.**
> 3. **Comment on the overall content of the speech.**

How spoken language is used in different contexts

You need to be aware of how spoken language changes in different situations, or **contexts**. There will be many differences between, for example, a conversation you have with a friend and a speech made by a politician.

In the workplace

You may have experience of work through a part-time job or through a work experience placement, which may give you some understanding of pressures on speech in the workplace.

> **How do work colleagues talk to each other? How would a boss and employee speak and behave towards one another? Create a brief role-play to explore your ideas and then listen to and / or watch a recording from a real workplace to gain a better idea.**

On television

Your experience of television is likely to include live programmes for children and young adults. It will probably also include live sports programmes and reality shows like *Strictly Come Dancing* and *The X Factor*.

> **Watch an episode of your favourite programme and make notes on how spoken language is used to make the programme interesting.**

For example:

> I enjoy listening to the panel arguing, more than watching the dancing. It seems spontaneous, but is also very well-rehearsed, or at least set-up.

In the classroom

You know this context well! Interactions in the classroom will much of the time include questions from both teachers and students. They can be used to quieten a class down, to make requests, to set a topic and to give commands.

> Could everybody listen now?
>
> What do you know about the works of Dickens?
>
> Please could you pass these books around so everyone gets one?

■ **How do students work together to learn well in the classroom?**
■ **How might a teacher skillfully use questions in the classroom?**

Record a classroom interaction, or observe talk in the classroom and take notes. Using the evidence you have, show the importance of questioning skills in the classroom.

Problem solving

Giving directions that are clear and reliable ought to be straightforward, but often is not. Explaining a procedure to someone can sometimes be very complicated, and you can make a complete mess of it. Making decisions can be difficult too, especially where two or more people have to agree.

Think of an example of a situation where someone might need to give directions. These could be directions for how to get somewhere or how to do something. Use notes, personal experience and memories to provide evidence. How do you think people could become better at everyday problem-solving, such as giving directions and making decisions?

EXAMINER'S TIP

■ When you write about spoken language, be free with your comments. If you think of something interesting to say about the way spoken language is used, write it down, because it will probably be relevant and will earn credit. The spoken language study is a specialist study where you are the specialist!

How spoken language is adapted to different listeners

In everyday life you adapt your spoken language when talking to different people. The way you speak may differ depending on the age of your listener, his or her authority or how formal the conversation is.

Talking to older or younger listeners

You will find yourself adapting your language when you talk to older and younger people. You may need to think about how much your listener knows about the subject you are talking about, or make your language simpler for young children.

> - **How do people speak and behave when talking and responding to primary school and pre-school children?**
> - **How do people speak and behave when talking and responding to elderly people?**
>
> **Use the evidence of recorded conversations and/or through close observation and note-taking.**

Responding to people in authority

The status and power of speakers may affect how they speak and behave. This balance of power may be affected by factors such as age, job, gender and context.

> **How do young people speak and behave when talking and responding to people in authority, such as a Head Teacher?**
>
> **Try to use evidence from your school life, work experience and life in the community to help you answer.**

Talking to friends and family

Most talk between friends and family members is informal and spontaneous because it is between people who know one another. However, even between friends and family, the formality of a conversation can differ. For example, parents may change what they say to each other when their children are around.

> **How do young people speak and behave when talking to and responding to friends and family?**
>
> **Use evidence from recordings, notes and recollections.**

Responding to 'unfamiliar adults'

Sometimes you may be unsure how formal to be when talking to someone unfamiliar. In these situations, you may need to remain relatively formal until you know what the tone of conversation will be. You don't want to risk being over-familiar with someone!

> **How do young people speak and behave when talking and responding to unfamiliar adults?**
>
> **Use evidence from transcripts and personal experience, and possibly examples from the media.**

Standard and non-standard forms of spoken language

Sometimes it is important to speak as correctly as possible. In other situations you can take a more relaxed attitude and speak in a non-standard way. This might be in local regional dialect, a youth dialect, or the speech of a specific group.

> - **How do you use non-standard English? Think of words you might use with your friends in place of standard words, such as 'good', 'bad', 'happy', etc.**
>
> - **How do people use non-standard spoken English positively in your community? Write down some specific examples.**

Controlled Assessment

The work in this unit should have helped you become more aware of the features of spoken language and issues affecting its use. You will be assessed for this part of the course by completing a task under Controlled Conditions. The task itself will be set by your teacher, and although you will be given time to prepare for and discuss the task before you write your response, as always the work that you produce must be your own. You will be allowed to take an annotated copy of your transcripts into the assessment with you, together with an A4 sheet of your own notes.

Tasks

Your task may be headed with a question like one of these below:

How does…?	How successful is…?	What are the strengths and weaknesses…?
Compare and contrast…		What are the problems experienced by…?
Examine closely the interview between…		What are the similarities and differences…?

Task support

You may also receive the following instructions:

Use the transcript, the recording, and any recollections of speech that are relevant to the task.

The task wording may include a number of bullet points that you could use as a checklist or even as the basis of your essay. For example:

Examine closely the interview…

You should consider:
- how the interviewer conducts the interview
- the questions asked
- what the interviewee says
- how the interviewee behaves
- your personal response to the interview as a whole.

You might get a two-part task, like the following:

> (i) Examine the transcript of the conversation between an employer and an employee.
> (ii) Write about any experiences you have had of dialogue between employers (or supervisors) and employees in the world of work.

A note on comparison

If you have a comparative task to answer like the one below, be extra careful to organize and signpost your thoughts carefully:

> Compare the dialogue from the novel…. with the transcript of spontaneous conversation between two friends.

If you are required to write at length about two transcripts, write about the first one in isolation, then write about the second, making links to the first transcript whenever they occur to you. You can add further comparisons at the end, if necessary.

If you are required to make a direct comparison between two small items, then make each point crisply and clearly. For example:

The interviewer looked the applicant straight in the eyes, but the interviewee looked down at the floor. The interviewer was obviously confident, whereas the interviewee was extremely nervous.

Controlled Assessment practice

Your Controlled Assessment task will be to write an essay on spoken language. All of your notes must be handed in with your final piece of writing.

Read the extract from an interview below. In this interview, a student, Joanna, attempts to persuade her council leader to provide funding for a local environmental project.

Joanna: I'm here on behalf of the Crewe Society for the Prevention of Cruelty for Animals and I'm basically... I've heard that you've had a sum of money that will be available to a certain charity and I'm here to tell you why I think the Crewe society should get that...

It was begun in the 1800's and ever since it's been devoted to promoting kindness to animals and preventing cruelty, but since it's still a charity it needs all the money it can get to keep it going and keep rescuing these injured animals and the Crewe branch is based at Saintley Grange.... and the wildlife hospital and Cattery there....... but these still need the donations to keep them running and the money would allow them to save more animals in the Crewe area, not just domestic animals but the wildlife too.

Because of all the new building work more animals' habitats are being destroyed and they need to be moved to safer areas and when the Sharington bypass was built a family of newts had to be moved from a pond because that pond was going to get destroyed and the money would allow new equipment to be bought for the wildlife hospital to do this, and I have a group of volunteers willing to build a Nature Reserve on an area of waste ground that would allow people to enjoy the wildlife and also it would be a safe place for the wildlife to be....

Councillor: Right, you're obviously very passionate about this, Joanna. Do you have friends that share the same interests as you, wanting to forward your cause?

Joanna: Yes, my sister also loves animals and she would be willing to help...

Councillor: Would she... right. So you think that we should be really seriously considering our area here for...

Joanna: Yes, because of all the new building work, the wildlife really needs to be saved... cos they are in danger from all the building ... cos building work doesn't really take into account the wildlife that would be hurt when it happens...

Councillor: They do take some measures, but I think you're right; we do lose a lot, don't we? Okay... What knowledge have you got about the kinds of projects, how do you know that giving five thousand pounds to this cause will improve the situation locally for us? Have you got any background knowledge from how things have worked in other areas?

Joanna: Well I know that in Northwich there is a big nature reserve that is very clean and it keeps wildlife free and safe... and people can walk through it and its right by the town centre and in a really quiet area of Northwich and that's worked really well.

Councillor: So that sounds like a similar project. How do you think funding has been used in that case to make the reserve successful?

Joanna: Well... I know that they had lots of people involved, who helped to plant trees and who go back regularly to keep the place tidy and remove litter – so most of the funding could be put towards adding new trees and nesting boxes and things like that. This brings more wildlife back to the area. They also put up signs about the wildlife there, which gets people more interested in it... once the reserve is set up, over time it will start to grow and it just needs a little bit of attention now and again to make sure that it is clear of rubbish.

Councillor: You have obviously done some research into this. How would you go about building this reserve?

Joanna: We would start by cleaning up the pool of water in the middle of the waste ground to create a safer habitat for pond life and then we would do a lot of re-planting... so we would need to buy plants and trees. We would also put in benches so local people can enjoy the reserve.

How effective is Joanna in persuading the councillor to agree to fund her chosen charity?

Look at:
• what she says
• how she says it
• how the interview is organized.

Sample answer

Read the extract from a spoken language study below, written about an interview between a council leader and a student who is seeking funding for a charity to help animals.

Student response

After watching Joanna in the video, I felt there were several aspects of her presentation that made her a strong candidate. She spoke clearly, and did not mumble, and nearly all of her speech was directed at the councillor, which made her seem confident in what she was saying.

There are areas where she could have gone into greater depth; for example, she could have explained how she personally became involved with the charity, and what projects are currently underway. She could also have given more examples of where money is desperately needed, and how the money will benefit the animals.

Joanna uses the word 'and' a lot, which makes her speech seem less structured and causes her to appear less prepared, as it suggests that she is saying something, and then remembering other things that she needs to say. This continues through the opening section, and may be the result of nerves, a bad habit, or both.

Some of the questions asked by the councillor did not help Joanna to extend her answers and fulfil her potential as fully as she might have been able to had the questions posed been more open. For example, the second question asked, regarding Joanna's friends, was a closed question, as it was very difficult for Joanna to expand her answer beyond 'yes' or 'no'. She had also partially answered this question in her introduction to the topic, as she mentioned that she already had 'a group of volunteers willing to build a nature reserve'.

EXAMINER'S COMMENT

You should take heart from this response, because as you can see, the writer is building a strong answer out of common-sense observations. She looks closely at what is said, but does not feel the need to write about every single word. She remains focused on the interaction between the interviewer and the interviewee. You do not need to be a technical expert to succeed!

How is spoken language assessed at GCSE?

Awareness of spoken language

Is there...

- ❑ limited awareness of how spoken language is used?
- ❑ some awareness of how speakers use spoken language?
- ❑ clear awareness of how spoken language is adapted?
- ❑ confident awareness of how spoken language is adapted?
- ❑ confident awareness of how spoken language is selected and adapted?

Influences

Is there...

- ❑ limited understanding of factors that influence spoken language?
- ❑ some understanding of the main influences on speakers' language choices?
- ❑ clear understanding of the different influences on speakers' language choices?
- ❑ sound understanding of significant influences on speakers' language choices?
- ❑ sophisticated understanding of subtle influences on speakers' language choices?

Speech variations

Is there...

- ❑ some ability to explain obvious differences in language?
- ❑ some ability to explain how differences in speech may affect communication?
- ❑ clear ability to explain the effects of speech variations?
- ❑ clear ability to explain the significance of speech variations?
- ❑ perceptive explanation of the impact of significant features of speech variations?

Language change

Is there...

- ❑ some ability to analyse and evaluate variations and changes in spoken language?
- ❑ some ability to analyse and evaluate how language changes?
- ❑ clear ability to analyse and evaluate effects of language changes?
- ❑ sustained ability to analyse and evaluate causes of variation and language change?

Preparing for Controlled Assessment

Here are the relevant details from the GCSE specification for this part of the assessment, including the relevant Assessment Objective for the English Language specification.

GCSE ENGLISH LANGUAGE UNIT 4: Spoken Language

Studying spoken language: variations, choices, change in spoken language (10%)

Controlled Assessment

You will need to write **one** written study of spoken language. This may contain more than one part.

AO2 Studying Spoken Language

- **Understand variations in spoken language, explaining why language changes in relation to contexts.**
  This means recognizing differences in spoken language and being able to explain why it changes in different situations.
- **Evaluate the impact of spoken language choices in your own and others' use.**
  This means that you can comment on your own and other people's use of spoken language, explaining the effect it can have on the listener.

Frequently asked questions

How long will I have to do the task?

You will write your final response in a two-hour Controlled Assessment in school or college. This time could be split into smaller sessions, as long as your teacher collects the work in at the end of each session. You will have time before this to do your research before taking the assessment.

What are the rules for research and planning?

During the research and planning stage, you have to work under limited supervision. You can team up with others in discussion groups and research activities, but you have to provide your own individual response for assessment. You may make use of research materials during the preparation period.

What can I take into the final assessment?

You will be allowed to take in one annotated copy of each transcript you are writing about and one A4 sheet of notes. The annotations and the sheet of notes must be **your own** work.

How much help can my teacher give me?

Your teacher can give you advice of a general kind during lessons, but is not allowed to give you direct feedback on your preparation. Your final piece of writing must be produced under formal supervision.

What should my final study look like?

It is fair to say that it should look like an essay; perhaps three to five sides of A4 paper, if you have average-sized handwriting. Make sure you include enough detail, but don't write pages and pages; remember you must keep your writing to the point!

How much is it worth?

The spoken language study is worth 10% of your marks in GCSE English Language.

How should I start to write my essay on the day?

Start with purpose and address the question. Don't waste your first paragraph on a long introduction.

Check your learning...

Now that you have reached the end of this chapter, look at the list of questions below and rate yourself on a scale of 1 to 4 on how well you feel you can perform each skill. '1' means you still have work to do while '4' means that you can perform it very well.

Can you...

✔ show that you understand how spoken language is used?

✔ show how people make choices in the way they speak?

✔ write an essay about some of the interesting challenges of using spoken language?

Acknowledgements

The publisher and author would like to thank the following for their permission to reproduce photographs and other copyright material:

P8l: Brand X Pictures/OUP; **p8tr:** David Lawrence/OUP; **p8br:** kret87/Shutterstock; **p10:** Buzz Pictures/Alamy; **p11:** Stockbyte/OUP; **p14:** Will Iredale/Shutterstock; **p15:** Phil Cole/Getty Images; **p16:** Rick Latham/EMPICS Entertainment; **p18:** Jeff J Mitchell/Getty Images; **p20:** Arthur Turner/Alamy; **p21:** Digital Vision/OUP; **p23:** Keith J Smith/Alamy; **p24:** Keith J Smith/Alamy; **p25t:** Patricia Fidi/Wikipedia: **p25b:** Ariadna de raaadt/Shutterstock; **p26t:** blickwinkel/Alamy; **p26b:** Patricia Fidi/Wikipedia; **p34:** D. Burke/OUP; **p37:** Volodymyr Pylypchuk/Shutterstock; **p38t:** Oleksii Abramov/Shutterstock; **p38b:** Mike Flippo/Shutterstock; **p39:** Bettmann/Corbis; **p40:** Vishnevskly Vasily/Shutterstock; **p41:** Daniel Gilbey Photography/Shutterstock; **p42:** Mikael Damkler/Shutterstock; **p44:** Jeff Morgan 07/Alamy; **p45:** Cynthia Farmer/Shutterstock; **p52:** Arielipma/Shutterstock; **p54l:** Trinity Mirror/Mirrorpix/Alamy, **p54tr:** Vladimir Wrangel/Shutterstock; **p54br:** Moviestore Collection Ltd/Alamy; **p59:** stewyphoto/Shutterstock; **p62:** Petro Feketa/Shutterstock; **p63:** Trinity Mirror/Mirrorpix/Alamy; **p65t:** Photos 12/Alamy; **p65b:** AF archive/Alamy; **p66:** Ian Tragen/Shutterstock; **p67:** Herwig Prammer/Reuters/Corbis; **p68:** Donald Cooper/Photostage; **p70:** Donald Cooper/Photostage; **p73:** Donald Cooper/Photostage.com; **p74t:** The Bridgeman Art Library; **p74l:** Rex Features; **p82:** Dean Mitchell/Shutterstock; **p84l:** Moviestore Collection Ltd/Alamy, **p84:** Moviestore Collection Ltd/Alamy; **p84r:** Terence/Shutterstock; **p85:** Joyfull/Shutterstock; **p86:** Dorothea Lange/Bettmann/Corbis; **p87:** R-Studio/Shutterstock; **p89:** MaleWitch/Shutterstock; **p90t:** Moviestore Collection Ltd/Alamy; **p90b:** AF archive/Alamy; **p91:** thefinalmiracle/Shutterstock; **p93:** J Tavin/Everett/Rex Features; **p94:** CBS/Getty Images; **p95:** AF Archive/Alamy; **p96:** Laurence Gough/Shutterstock; **p101:** Tatiana Popova/Shutterstock; **p104l:** Larry Lilac/Alamy; **p104c:** AF archive/Alamy; **p104r:** Donald Cooper/Photostage; **p105:** Anita Patterson Peppers/Shutterstock; **p107:** AF archive/Alamy; **p108:** Paul Lovelace/Rex Features; **p110:** Miroslaw Dzladkowlec/Shutterstock; **p111:** Alexey Lebedev/Shutterstock; **p112:** Donald Cooper/Photostage; **p116:** Donald Cooper/Photostage; **p117:** AF archive/Alamy; **p118t:** Donald Cooper/Photostage; **p118b:** EDHAR/Shutterstock; **p119:** tapgoodimages/Shutterstock; **p122:** Thomas SkjÃ?Â¡veland/Shutterstock; **p123:** Everett Collection/Rex Features; **p134:** Supri Suharjoto/Shutterstock; **p137:** Janaka Dharmasena/Shutterstock; **p138:** Colin Palmer Photography/OUP; **p139:** Stephen Aaron Rees/Shutterstock; **p140:** Corel/OUP; **p141:** Michael Woodruff/Shutterstock; **p142:** Corbis/OUP; **p144:** M. Bonotto/Shutterstock; **p146:** S.M./Shutterstock; **p147:** Rafael Ramirez Lee/Shutterstock; **p148:** Vadim Kozlovsky/Shutterstock; **p149:** Valueline/OUP; **p150:** Zoran Karapancev/Shutterstock; **p152t:** Image Source/OUP; **p152b:** Yellowj/Shutterstock; **p153:** ene/Shutterstock; **p154:** Damian Palus/Shutterstock; **p.155:** Images of Birmingham Premium/Alamy; **p160:** Yuri Arcurs/Shutterstock; **p162tl:** Peter1977/Shutterstock; **p162tr:** Tanya Ien/Shutterstock; **p162bc:** Alexander Raths/Shutterstock; **p163:** Pierre-Yves Babelon/Shutterstock; **p164:** discpicture/Shutterstock; **p165:** Chris Cooper-Smith/Alamy; **p165b:** Jose Gil/Shutterstock; **p166:** Image Source/OUP; **p167:** ultimathule/Shutterstock; **p168:** Peter Guess/Shutterstock; **p169:** Andrr/Shutterstock; **p170:** Tsian/Shutterstock; **p171:** 1000 words/Shutterstock; **p172:** Pres Panayotov/Shutterstock; **p173:** L. Watcharapol/Shutterstock; **p175:** Yuri Arcurs/Shutterstock; **p177:** David Davis/Shutterstock; **p178t:** Stephane Cardinale/People Avenue/Corbis; **p178l:** Margaret Smeaton/Alamy; **p179:** Julija Sapic/Shutterstock; **p180:** Jarrod Boord/Shutterstock; **p182:** Daniel Yordanov/Shutterstock; **p188t:** Monkey Business Images/Shutterstock; **p188b:** michaeljung/Shutterstock; **p191:** Lasse Kristensen/Shutterstock; **p193l:** Dean Mitchell/Shutterstock, **p193b:** Laurence Gough/Shutterstock; **p194:** Diego Cervo/Shutterstock; **p195:** 1000 Words/Shutterstock; **p196t:** Barone Firenze; **p196b:** Sergei Telegin/Shutterstock; **p198:** Paul M Thompson/Alamy; **p199:** Scoutingstock/Shutterstock;

p201: Galushko Sergey/Shutterstock; **p202:** Frances Roberts/Alamy; **p203:** StockLite/Shutterstock; **p204:** Kuznetsov Alexey/Shutterstock; **p207:** Yuri Arcurs/Shutterstock; **p208:** Simone van den Berg/Shutterstock; **p210l:** Stockbroker/OUP; **p210c:** OUP; **p210r:** Comstock/OUP; **p211:** Good Shoot/OUP; **p213:** Linda Flynn/Shutterstock; **p214t:** Image Source/OUP; **p214b:** Upper Cut/OUP; **p216:** Rex Features; **p217:** Rex Features; **p219:** Photodisc/OUP; **p220:** Photodisc/OUP; **p222:** Brand X Pictures/OUP.

Illustrations by: Mark Brierley, Ray and Corinne Burrows, Martin Saunders, Rory Walker.

The publisher and author are grateful for permission to reprint the following copyright material:

Extracts taken from 'Fire Safety in the Home', leaflet no FSO69 (2007), Crown © 2007, are used under the terms of the Open Government Licence; **Maya Angelou:** 'Woman Work' from *The Complete Collected Poems of Maya Angelou* (Virago, 1994, 1995, 1996), and extract from *I Know Why the Caged Bird Sings* (Virago, 1984), reprinted by permission of Virago, an imprint of Little Brown Book Group; **Belfast Telegraph:** 'Snow joke: Riot police rapped for sledding on shields', *Belfast Telegraph*, 15.1.2010; **Berlie Doherty:** 'Playgrounds' from *Walking on Air* (Hodder Children's Books, 1999) copyright © Berlie Doherty 1993, reprinted by permission of David Higham Associates; **Roddy Doyle:** extracts from *Paddy Clarke Ha Ha Ha* (Secker & Warburg, 1993), reprinted by permission of The Random House Group Ltd; **U A Fanthorpe:** line from 'You will be hearing from us shortly' from *New and Collected Poems 1978-2003* (Enitharmon Press, 2010), reprinted by permission of R V Bailey; **Guardian News and Media Ltd:** Georgia Brown: 'Why can't we cope with snow?', *The Guardian*, 8.2.2007, copyright © Guardian News and Media Ltd 2007; **Brian Jones:** 'About Friends' from *Spitfire on the Northern Line* (Chatto & Windus, 1994), reprinted by permission of The Random House Group Ltd; **Harper Lee:** extract from *To Kill a Mockingbird* (Wm Heinemann 1960/Vintage 2004), reprinted by permission of The Random House Group Ltd; **Ian McMillan:** 'In the End, it's the Hope...', copyright © Ian McMillan 29010, 19.06.2010 for BBC Broadcasting House (Radio 4), reprinted by permission of the author c/o UK Touring; **Brian Patten:** 'Sometimes it Happens' from *And Sometimes it Happens*, a Broadsheet published by Ralph Steadman (Steam Press, 1972), reprinted by permission of Rogers Coleridge & White Ltd, 20 Powis Mews, London Wll 1JN; **Pembroke Castle Trust:** extract from homepage of their website www.pembroke-castle.co.uk; **Siegfried Sassoon:** 'Base Details' and line from 'The Hero' from *The War Poems* (Faber, 2006), copyright © Siegfried Sassoon, reprinted by permission of the Estate of George Sassoon c/o Barbara Levy Literary Agency; **The Scout Association:** extract from an old recruiting advertisement. To find out more, visit www.scouts.org.uk or call 0845 300 1818; **John Steinbeck:** extract from *Of Mice and Men* (Penguin Classics, 2006), copyright © John Steinbeck 1937, 1965, reprinted by permission of Penguin Books Ltd; **St Helena Government:** extract from Facebook petition page: 'Join the Airport for St Helena Group'; **Allan Stratton:** opening extract from **Chandra's Secret** (Annick Press, 2004), reprinted by permission of the UK publishers, Chicken House Ltd and of Annick Press, Canada; **Matthew Sweeney:** 'Only the Wall' from *Fatso in the Red Suit* (Faber, 1995), reprinted by permission of Faber & Faber Ltd; **Meera Syal:** extracts from *Anita and Me* (Flamingo, 1997), copyright © Meera Syal 1996, reprinted by permission of HarperCollins Publishers Ltd; **Benjamin Zephaniah:** 'Talking Turkeys' from *Talking Turkeys* (Puffin, 1995), copyright © Benjamin Zephaniah 1994, reprinted by permission of Penguin Books Ltd.

Although we have made every effort to trace and contact all copyright holders before publication this has not been possible in all cases. If notified, the publisher will rectify any errors or omissions at the earliest opportunity.